AF538503

AN INTRODUCTION TO EXPERIMENTAL ASTRONOMY

ROGER B. CULVER
Colorado State University

AN OBSERVATIONAL WORKBOOK

W. H. FREEMAN AND COMPANY
New York

To Kenny, Kathleen, and Larry
with love

Library of Congress Cataloging in Publication Data

Culver, Roger B.
An introduction to experimental astronomy.

1. Astronomy — Experiments. I. Title.
QB62.7.C84 1983 522 83-9050
ISBN 0-7167-1495-7

Copyright © 1974, 1984 by W. H. Freeman and Company

No part of this book may be reproduced by any mechanical, photographic, or electronic process, or in the form of a phonograph recording, nor may it be stored in a retrieval system, transmitted, or otherwise copied for public or private use, without written permission from the publisher.

ISBN: 0-7167-1495-7

Printed in the United States of America

5 6 7 8 9 0 WC 9 9 8 7 6 5 4 3 2 1 0

TABLE OF CONTENTS

CREDITS FOR ILLUSTRATIONS

FIGURE	SOURCE
1.1	U.S. Army Signal Corps
2.1	Black Star Publishing Co., Inc.
5.1	Enok Jonsson, *Sky and Telescope*
5.2	Jean Dragesco, *Sky and Telescope*
7.1	Yerkes Observatory
7.2	Lick Observatory
10.1	Leander McCormick Observatory
10.2	Kitt Peak National Observatory
11.1	Kitt Peak National Observatory
11.2	Kitt Peak National Observatory
12.2	The Hale Observatories
14.1	The Hale Observatories
14.2	The University of Michigan Observatories
15.1	The Hale Observatories
16.1	Copyright National Geographic Society—Palomer Observatory Sky Survey
17.1	The Hale Observatories
19.1	The Hale Observatories
20.1	Lick Observatory
21.1	Kitt Peak National Observatory Publications of the Astronomical Society of the Pacific
22.1	Lick Observatory
22.2	Copyright National Geographic Society—Palomar Observatory Sky Survey

All other photographs in this manual that are not listed here are from the Colorado State University Observatory.

PREFACE

Although astronomy, the oldest of the observational sciences, has experienced a significant increase of student interest in recent years, the number and variety of laboratory experiments and exercises available to the elementary astronomy instructor has remained relatively small. It is hoped that the exercises presented herein will alleviate this situation to some extent and provide the student with a solid introduction to a reasonable cross section of the concepts and methods employed by astronomers in their relentless pursuit of the often elusive secrets of the night sky.

In any undertaking of this type, the author must, of necessity, rely heavily on assistance from others. In addition to those individuals and institutions listed in the picture credits who so kindly permitted the use of various photographs and illustrations appearing in this manual, the author would like to express his deepest appreciation and gratitude to Mr. Ken Flurchick, who in the course of braving the Astronomy 100 laboratory sections at Colorado State University, has made a number of valuable suggestions and corrections to this text, to Ms. Mary Spencer who, in her typically quiet and competent way, has transformed yet another one of my illegible manuscripts into a coherent presentation, to all of the skilled individuals from the CSU Office of Instructional Services, without whose abilities the photographs and illustrations which form the backbone of this text would not have been possible, to all of those instructors of laboratory astronomy courses who, over the past several years, have taken time out to offer their cogent advice and criticisms, and especially to all of the students who have labored through these exercises and in the process have offered many excellent suggestions for their improvement.

Roger B. Culver
March, 1981

Experiment 1

A Determination of the Speed of Light

I. Introduction

One of the most fundamental constants of nature is the speed at which electromagnetic radiation, including visible light, propagates through free space. Because of its very large numerical value, it was not until late in the seventeenth century that this constant was evaluated with any degree of accuracy. Since that time, scientists have devised a number of methods to measure this constant with ever greater precision. In this exercise you will determine the speed of light by simultaneously measuring the lunar trigonometric parallax and the radar travel time to and from the moon.

II. Measurements

On the radar trace shown in Figure 1.1, determine the time t_i of the initial transmission (tall sharp peak) and the echo time t_e (short, broad peak). Remove Figures 1.2 and 1.3 from your text and superimpose the two photographs in such a way that the lunar features are exactly aligned with each other. With the photographs thus adjusted, measure the distance d_* between the two star images (black dots) and the length d_o of the 480" scaling line. Be sure that d_* and d_o are measured in the same units of length. Enter all of your measurements in your data sheet.

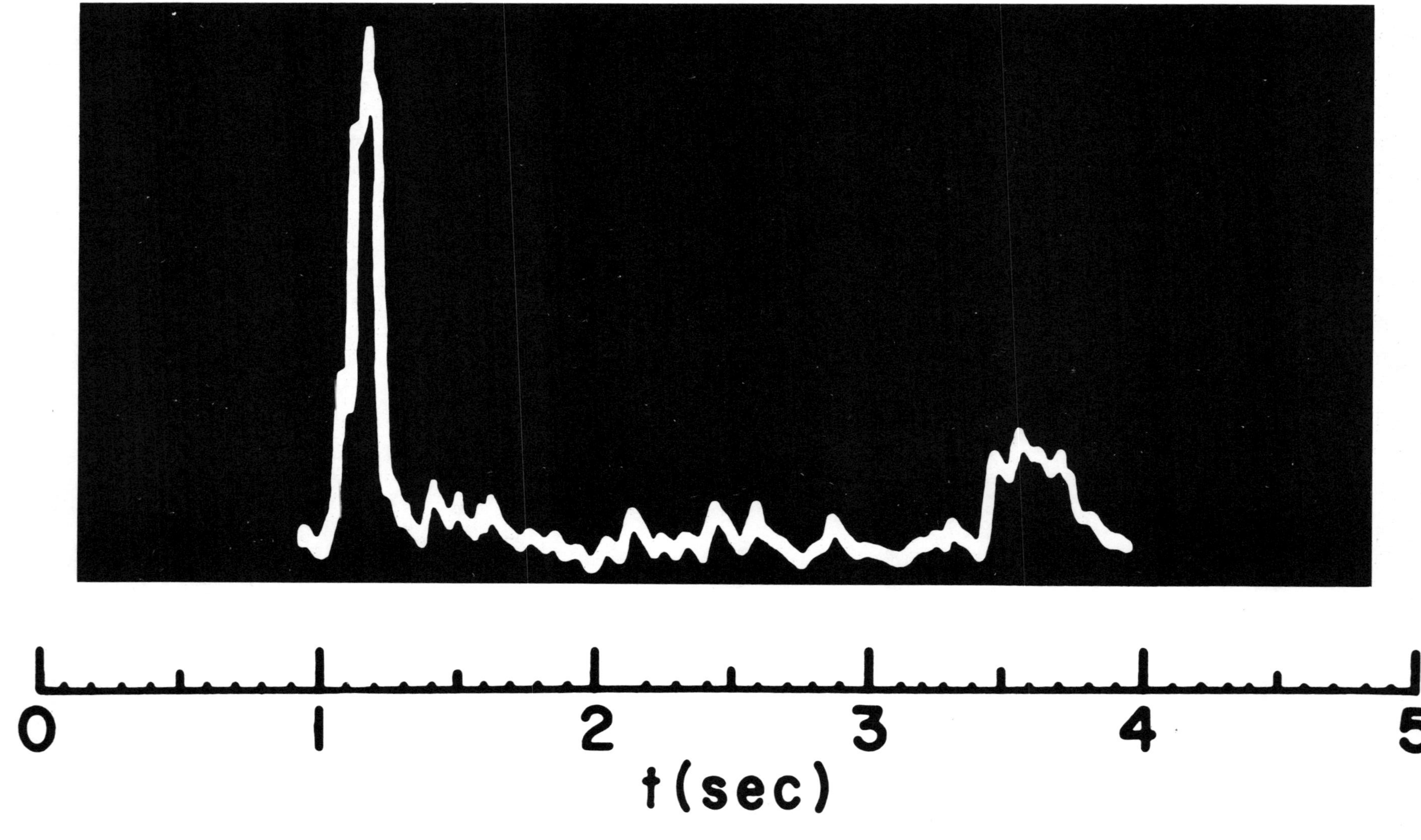

FIGURE 1.1

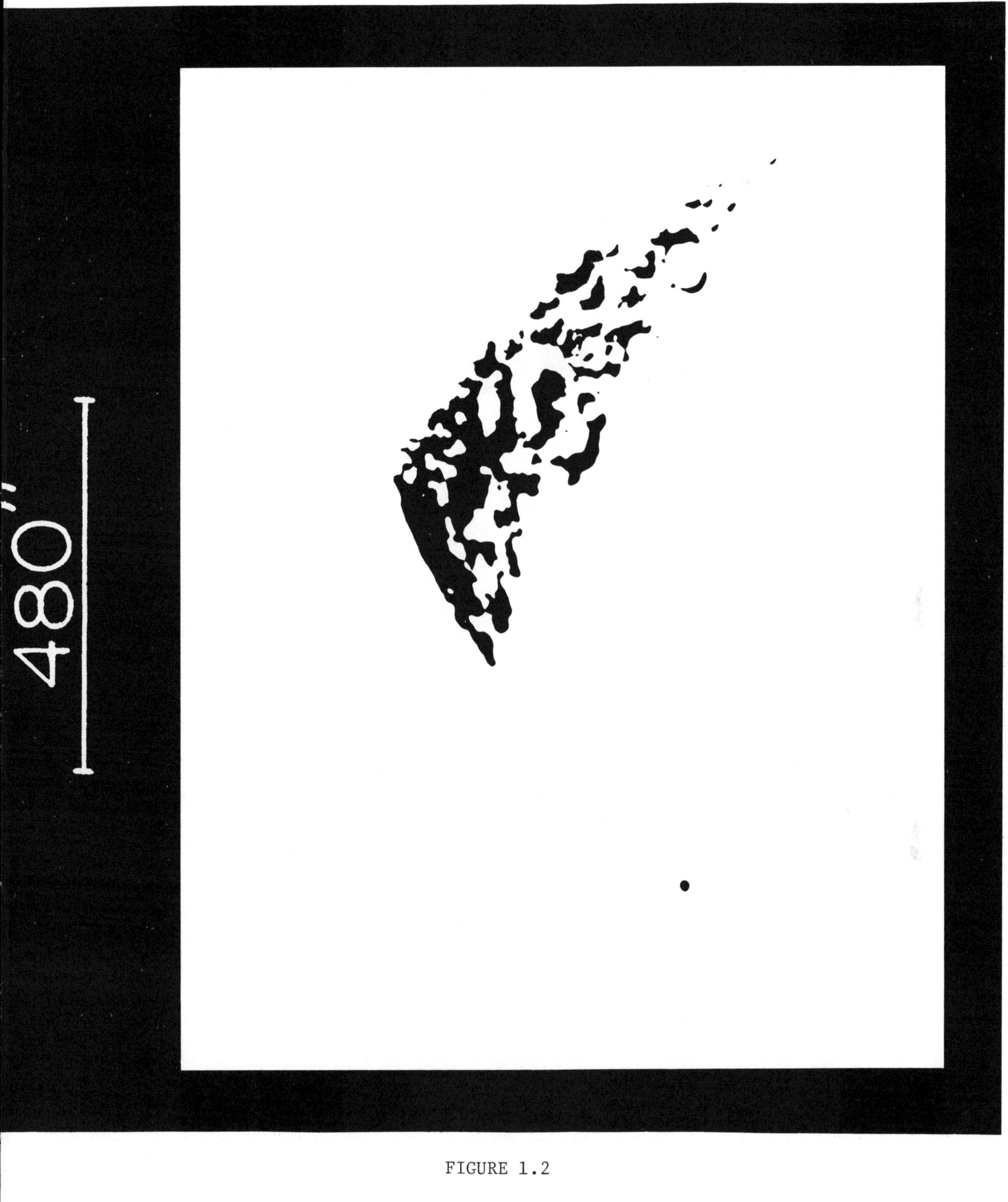

FIGURE 1.2

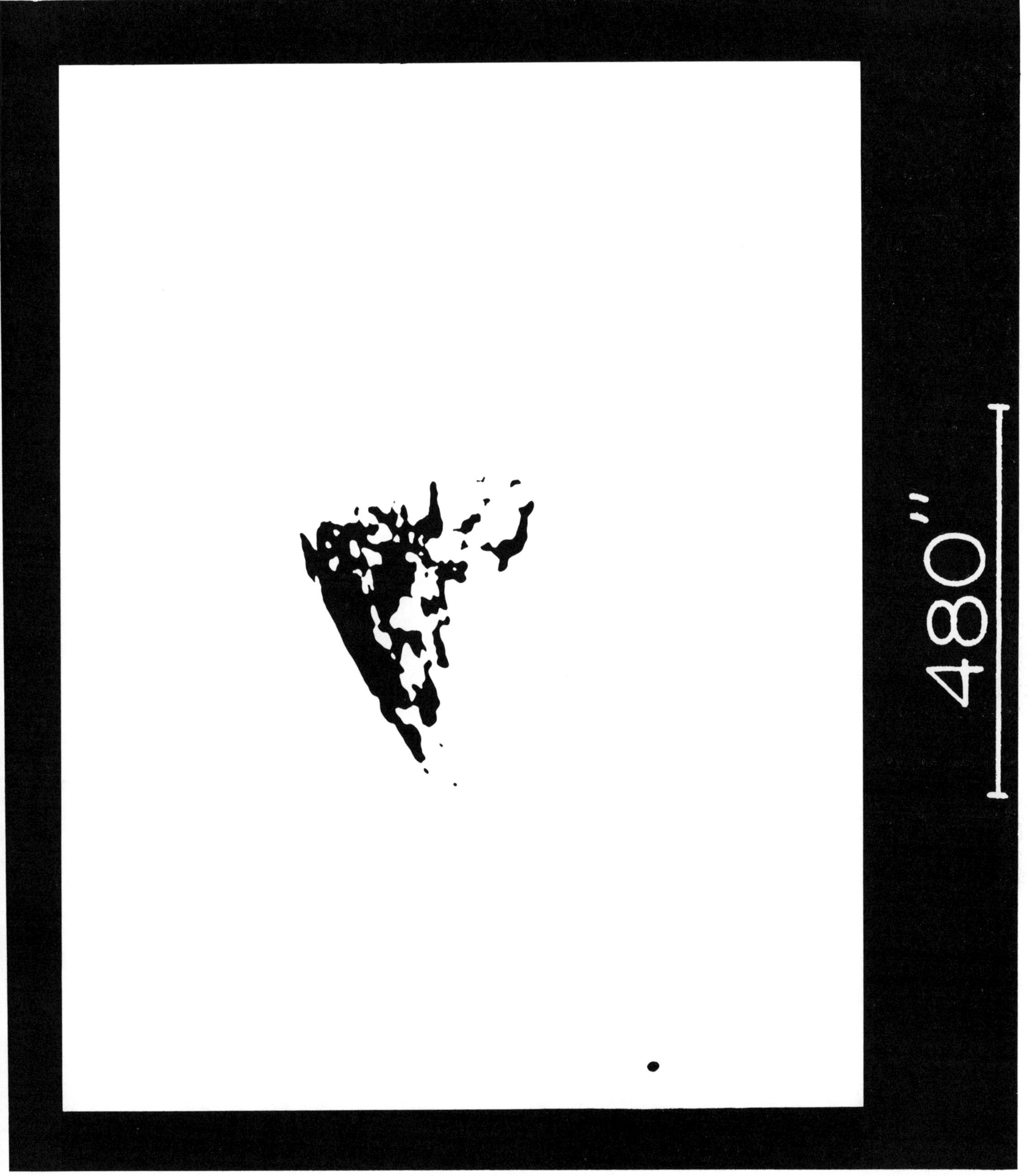

FIGURE 1.3

III. Reductions

Calculate the lunar parallax α in arcseconds (") from your measured values of d_* and d_o using

$$(1.1) \quad \alpha = 480'' \, (d_*/d_o)$$

The distance r to the moon should then be computed using the relationship

$$(1.2) \quad r = \frac{206265 \, D}{\alpha}$$

where D is the distance between the observers who took the photographs in Figure 1.2 and 1.3 and is equal to 183 km.

Determine the travel time $\Delta t = t_e - t_i$ it takes for the radar echo to return to the earth, and then calculate the speed of light c using

$$(1.3) \quad c = \frac{2r}{\Delta t}$$

IV. Questions

1. Explain why the star in Figure 1.2 is located at a different spot relative to the moon's edge than the star in Figure 1.3.

2. Explain Equation (1.3).

3. Discuss two basic assumptions which have been made in this experiment.

Data Sheet

t_i

t_e

Δt

d_*

d_o

α

$D = 183$ km

r

c

Experiment 2

Positional Astronomy

I. Introduction

One of the important aspects of experimental astronomy is the field of astrometry or the precise determination of the positions of objects on the celestial sphere. To this end, astronomers usually employ the so-called equatorial system in which the position of an object is expressed in two coordinates: the declination or angular distance of an object north or south of the celestial equator, and the right ascension or the angular distance east of the vernal equinox point as measured along the celestial equator. In this exercise you will determine the right ascension and declination of the sun by observing the variation of its angular distance above the horizon (altitude) as a function of time over a 24 hour period.

II. Measurements

On each of the photographs of the midnight sun shown in Figure 2.1, measure the distance x_s between the sun's center and the horizon which can be assumed to be the same as the sea level. In the same units measure the length x_o of the 10° scaling line. Enter all of your results in your data sheet.

III. Reductions

Calculate the altitude a_s of the sun for each of the

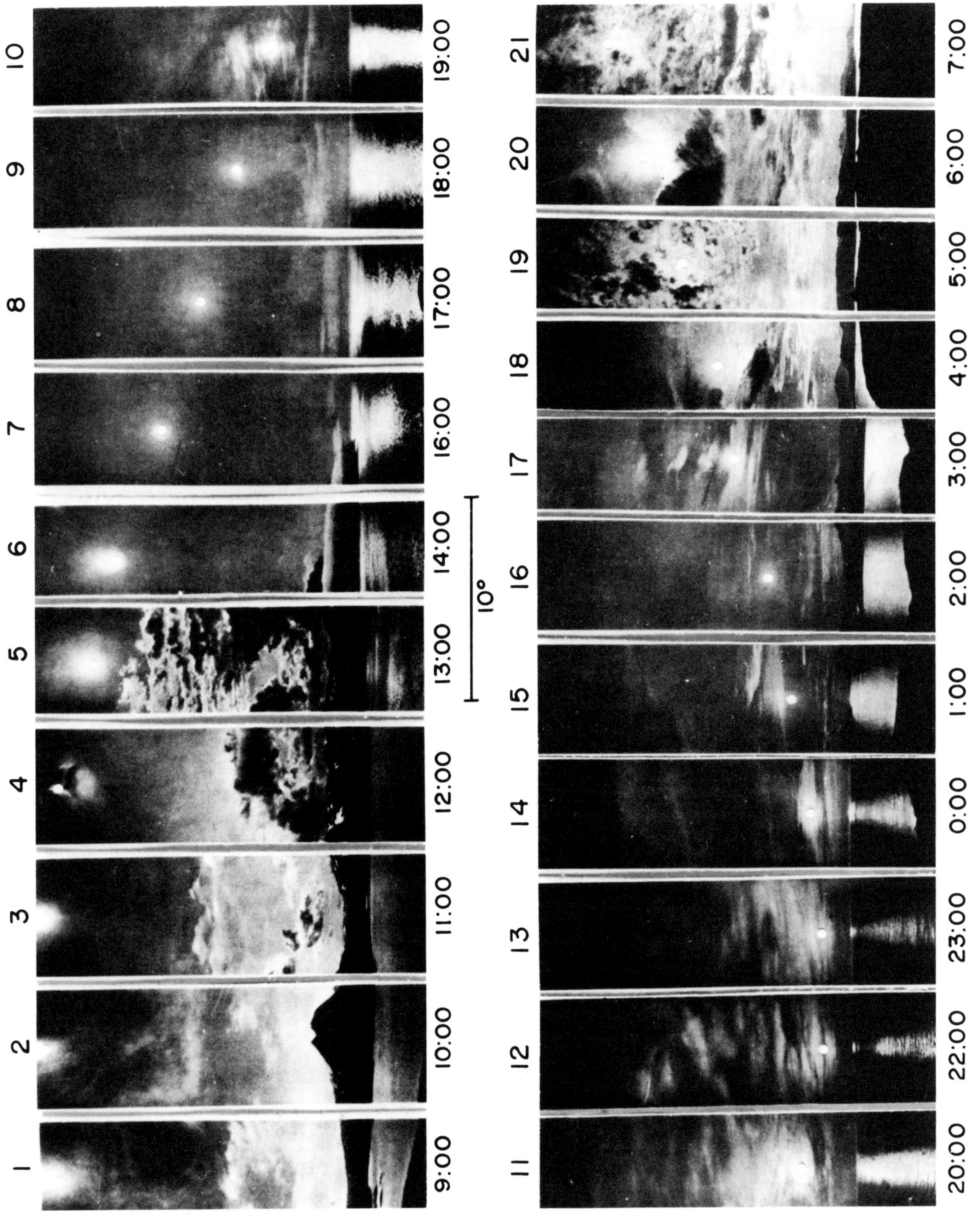

1
9:00
2
10:00
3
11:00
4
12:00
5
13:00
6
14:00
7
16:00
8
17:00
9
18:00
10
19:00
10°
11
20:00
12
22:00
13
23:00
14
0:00
15
1:00
16
2:00
17
3:00
18
4:00
19
5:00
20
6:00
21
7:00

FIGURE 2.1

photographs shown in Figure 2.1, using the relation

$$(2.1) \quad a_s(\text{degrees}) = 10° \frac{x_s}{x_o}$$

and enter your results in your data sheet. Plot a_s versus the sidereal time and pass a smooth curve through the resulting points. Read off the values of the maximum altitude a_{max} and the minimum altitude a_{min} as well as their corresponding times t_{max} and t_{min}. Calculate the declination of the sun $\delta_\odot$ from the relation

$$(2.2) \quad \delta_\odot = \frac{a_{max} + a_{min}}{2} \quad .$$

The right ascension of the sun $\alpha_\odot$ is numerically equal to the sidereal time of the sun's maximum altitude or

$$(2.3) \quad \alpha_\odot = t_{max} \quad .$$

Find $\alpha_\odot$ and $\delta_\odot$ and enter your results in your data sheet.

IV. Questions

1. Discuss the shape of the a_s versus t plot you obtained in this exercise. What would the plot look like if you were at the earth's equator?

2. Show by means of diagrams why $\delta_{\odot}$ is the mean of the sun's maximum and minimum altitudes. Why is $\alpha_{\odot}$ equal to the sidereal time of the maximum solar altitude?

3. Discuss how one's latitude and longitude on the earth could be determined from these data, assuming that the sidereal time of the Greenwich meridian (longitude = 0°) were known.

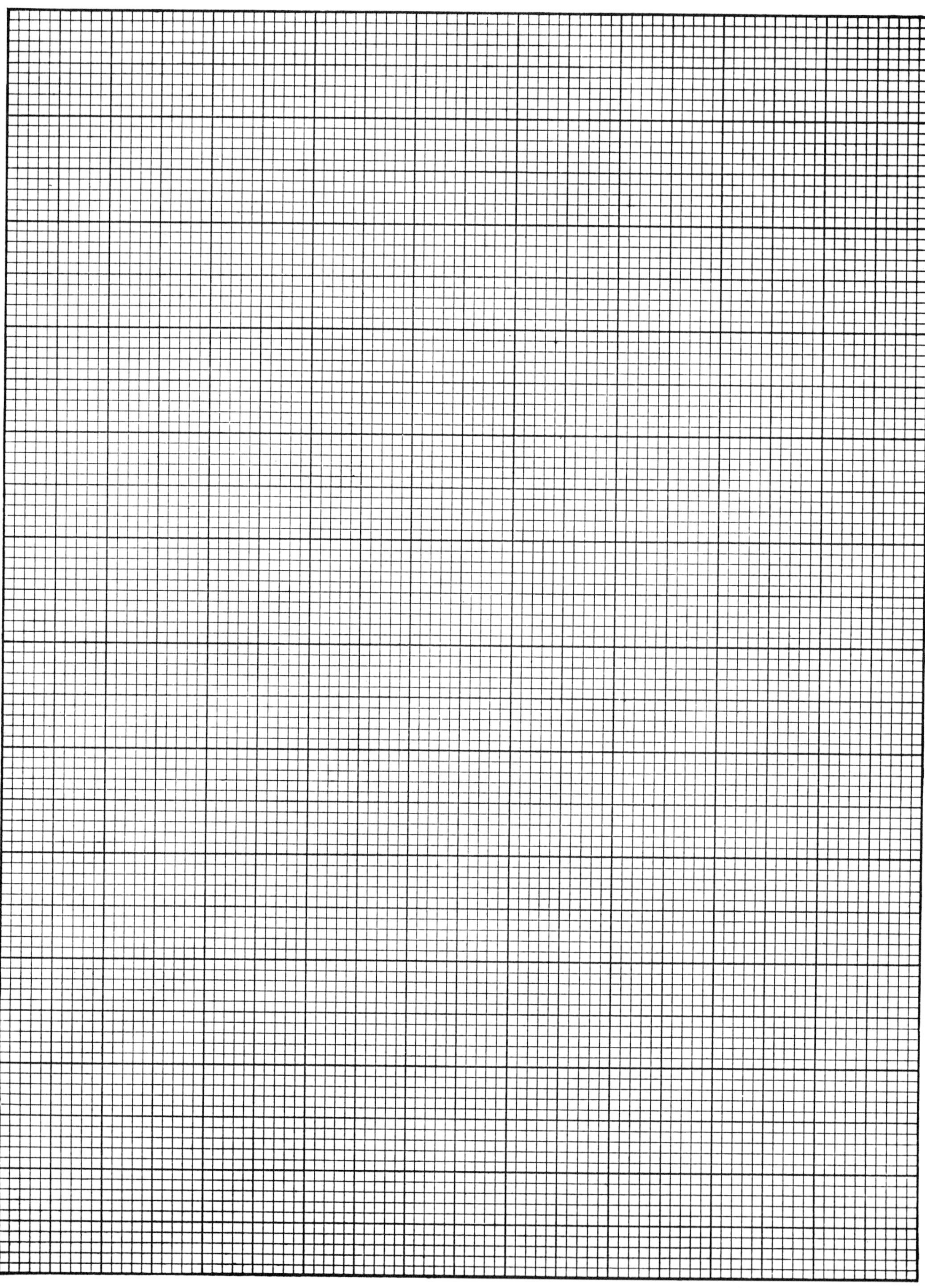

Data Sheet

Plate	x_s	a_s	Plate	x_s	a_x
1			12		
2			13		
3			14		
4			15		
5			16		
6			17		
7			18		
8			19		
9			20		
10			21		
11					

x_o

a_{max}

a_{min}

t_{max}

$\delta_{\odot}$

$\alpha_{\odot}$

Experiment 3

Photometric Astronomy

I. Introduction

The branch of observational astronomy that deals with the measurement of the brightness of celestial objects is known as photometric astronomy. In order to facilitate such measurements, astronomers have developed a brightness rating scale or "scale of magnitudes" in which the ratio of apparent brightnesses ℓ_1/ℓ_2 of two objects is related to their respective magnitudes m_1 and m_2 by the following equation;

$$(3.1) \quad m_1 - m_2 = -2.5 \log_{10}\{\ell_1/\ell_2\}$$

In this system, the zero point is roughly equal to the mean brightness of the ten most prominent stars in the night sky.

These magnitudes can be measured visually, photographically, or photoelectrically. In this exercise, you will make a determination of the magnitude of a star by photographic means.

II. Measurements

On the photograph of the Hyades region of Taurus shown in Figure 3.1, locate each of the stars listed in Table 3.1 as well as the unknown star indicated by your instructor using the finder chart shown in Figure 3.2. Carefully measure the diameter d_* of each star image by measuring a given image across several different diameters and averaging the results. The measurements should be

FIGURE 3.1

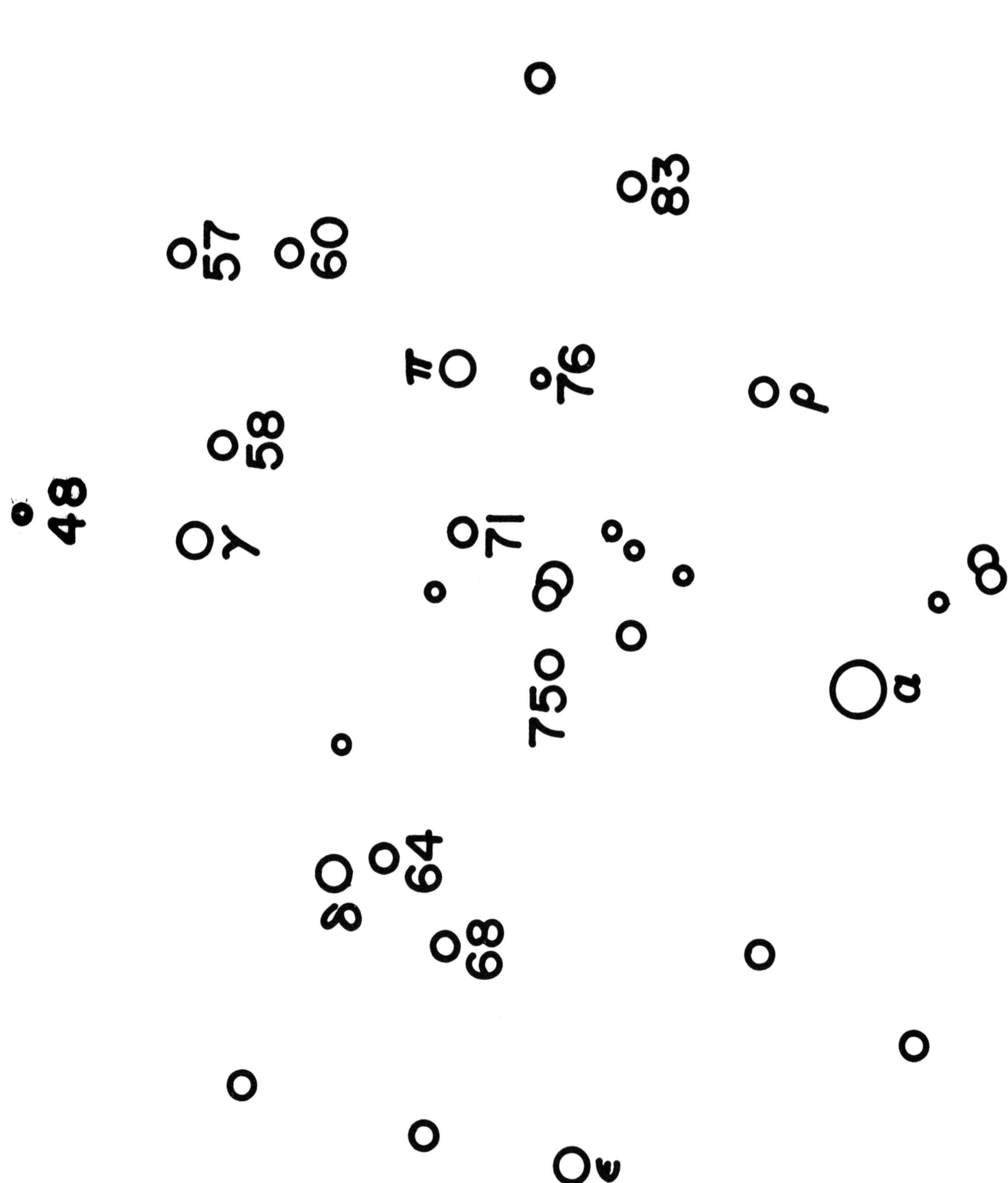

FIGURE 3.2

accurate to at least ±0.2 mm. Enter all of your results in your data sheet.

III. Reductions

Calculate ${d_*}^2$ for each of your reference stars as well as the corresponding values for $\log_{10} {d_*}^2$. Plot $\log_{10} {d_*}^2$ versus the corresponding B magnitude for each of your reference stars and pass a straight line through the resulting set of points. This straight line represents the calibration curve for the star field. Calculate $\log_{10} {d_*}^2$ for your unknown star and read off the corresponding B value from your calibration curve. Enter the results in your data sheet.

Table 3.1

Magnitude Data for the Comparison Stars

Star	B Magnitude
α Tau	+ 2.39
ε Tau	+ 4.56
ρ Tau	+ 4.90
58 Tau	+ 5.48
48 Tau	+ 6.72

IV. Questions

1. Discuss the advantages and disadvantages of measuring the brightness of celestial objects by photographic means as compared with visual and photoelectric techniques.

2. Why would you expect the plot of $\log_{10} d_*^2$ versus the B magnitude to result in a straight line?

3. Why do you suppose that the B or blue magnitude is used in this exercise instead of the visual magnitude V?

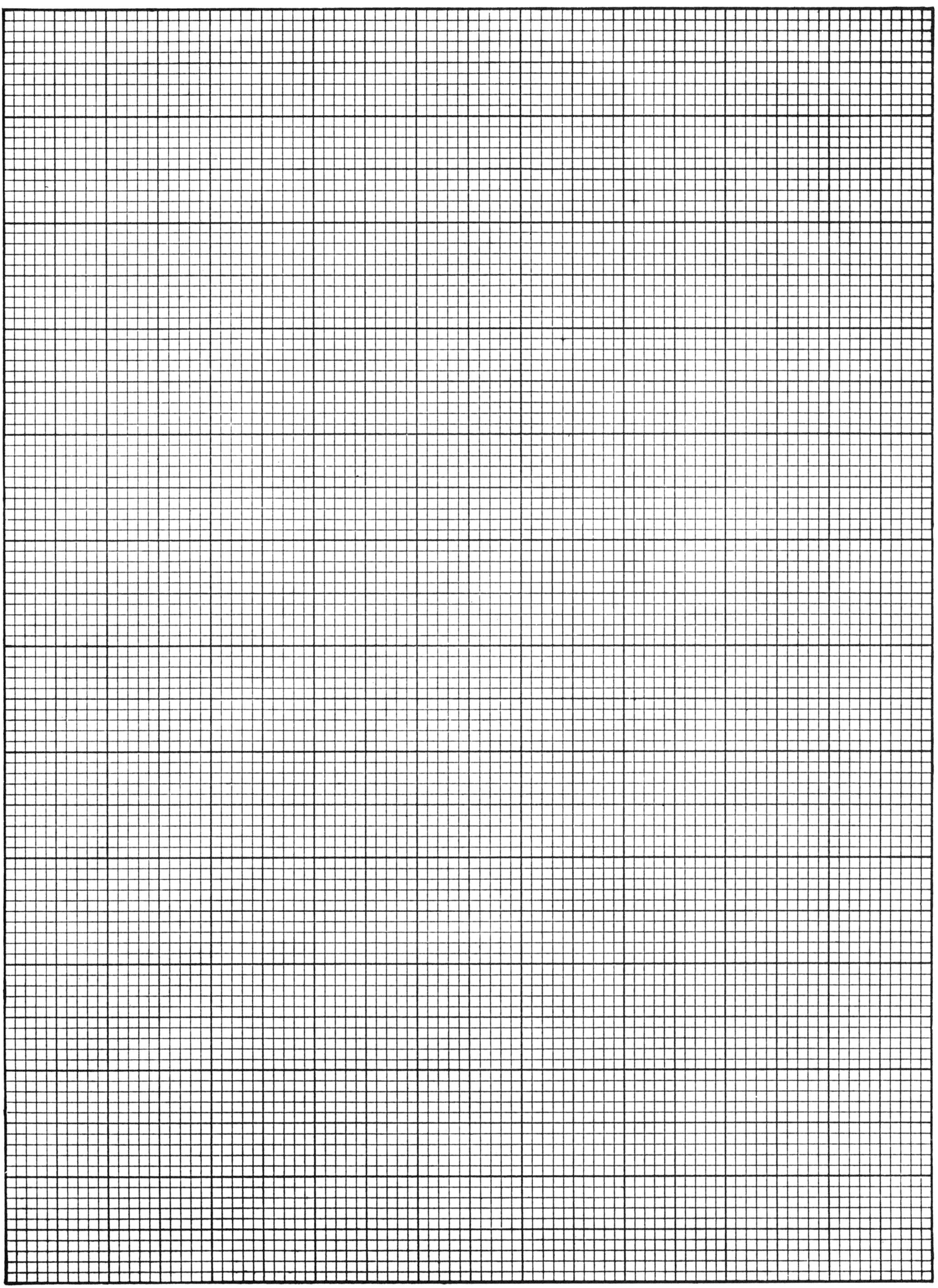

Data Sheet

Star	B	d_* (mm)	d_*^2 (mm^2)	$\log_{10}(d_*^2)$
α Tau	+ 2.39			
ε Tau	+ 4.56			
ρ Tau	+ 4.90			
58 Tau	+ 5.48			
48 Tau	+ 6.72			
Unknown Star				

Experiment 4

The Trans-Uranian Planet

I. Introduction

Perhaps the greatest triumph of Newtonian mechanics came in 1846 when the existence of the planet Neptune was successfully predicted solely on the basis of its gravitational effect on the motion of the planet Uranus. In this exercise you will carry out a simplified version of this calculation.

II. Data

The basic data for this exercise are presented in Table 4.1 in which an unaccounted for discrepancy in the motion of the planet Uranus is tabulated as a function of time and heliocentric longitude from 1720 to 1840.

III. Reductions

Plot the discrepancy Δ versus its corresponding time and pass a smooth curve through the resulting points. Determine the times t_1 and t_2 at which the Δ versus t plot passes through either a maximum or minimum value. If S_N is the synodic period of Neptune as seen from Uranus, then we have

$$(4.1) \quad S_N = 2\,|t_2 - t_1|$$

and thus Neptune's sidereal period P_N is then

$$(4.2) \quad P_N = \frac{S_N P_U}{S_N - P_U}$$

where P_U is the sidereal period of Uranus and is equal to 84.02 years. Applying Kepler's Harmonic Law, we obtain a_N, the mean distance between Neptune and the sun

$$(4.3) \quad a_N = \sqrt[3]{P_N^2}$$

Calculate Neptune's synodic period, sidereal period, and mean distance using Equations (4.1), (4.2), and (4.3), and enter your results in your data sheet.

The mean heliocentric angular velocity ω_N of Neptune can be written as

$$(4.4) \quad \omega_N = \frac{360°}{P_N}$$

and the heliocentric longitude λ_t of Neptune at any time t is given by

$$(4.5) \quad \lambda_t = \lambda_o + \omega_N(t_I - t_o)$$

where λ_o is the longitude of Uranus at the point where the Δ versus t plot passes through a maximum value, t_o is the corresponding time of the maximum value, and t_I is the time assigned to you by your instructor. All t values should be in years. Calculate λ_t from Equation (4.5) and enter the result in your data sheet. The date that Neptune is in opposition to the sun as seen from the earth and hence would be at its brightest expected magnitude is given by

$$(4.6) \quad \text{Date of Opposition} = \text{September } 22 + \frac{\lambda_t}{0.98°/\text{day}}$$

Find the date of opposition from Equation (4.6) and enter your results in your data sheet. Assuming that Neptune lies on the ecliptic, also calculate the right ascension α_N and declination δ_N of Neptune by interpolating the data in Table 4.2 where $\lambda = \lambda_t$.

Table 4.1. The Motion of Uranus

Year	$\Delta_{\text{Obs-Theory}}$	λ
1720	-30"	196°
1731	-50	244
1735	-50	261
1737	-54	270
1740	-53	283
1750	-52	326
1753	-49	339
1756	-50"	352°
1764	-38	26
1769	-21	48
1780	+ 3	96
1783	+ 8	109
1786	+12	121
1789	+18	134
1792	+17"	146°
1795	+20	159
1807	+29	209
1810	+30	222
1813	+31	235
1816	+34	248
1819	+31	261
1823	+32"	278°
1825	+35	287
1828	+34	300
1831	+36	313
1834	+35	326
1837	+34	339
1840	+31	352

Table 4.2. The Right Ascensions and Declinations of Selected Points on the Ecliptic

λ	α	δ
0°	0^h00^m	00°00'
20	1 16	+08 00
40	2 30	+14 49
60	3 52	+20 12
80	5 18	+23 06
90°	6^h00^m	+23°27'
100	6 45	+23 02
120	8 11	+20 03
140	9 32	+14 38
160	10 46	+07 53
180	12^h00^m	00°00'
200	13 14	-07 49
220	14 30	-14 47
240	15 51	-20 10
260	17 18	-23 05
270°	18^h00^m	-23°27'
280	18 43	-23 04
300	20 10	-20 06
320	21 28	-14 57
340	22 45	-07 55

IV. Questions

1. What assumptions regarding the "unknown" planet have been made in this exercise? To what extent are these assumptions true?

2. Why can we assert that Uranus, Neptune, and the sun are lined up at about the same time when the Δ versus t plot passes through a maximum or minimum value? When would Uranus and Neptune be closest to each other? When would they be farthest away? Explain.

3. Why do you suppose that you were asked to calculate the date of Neptune's opposition as well as its position on that date?

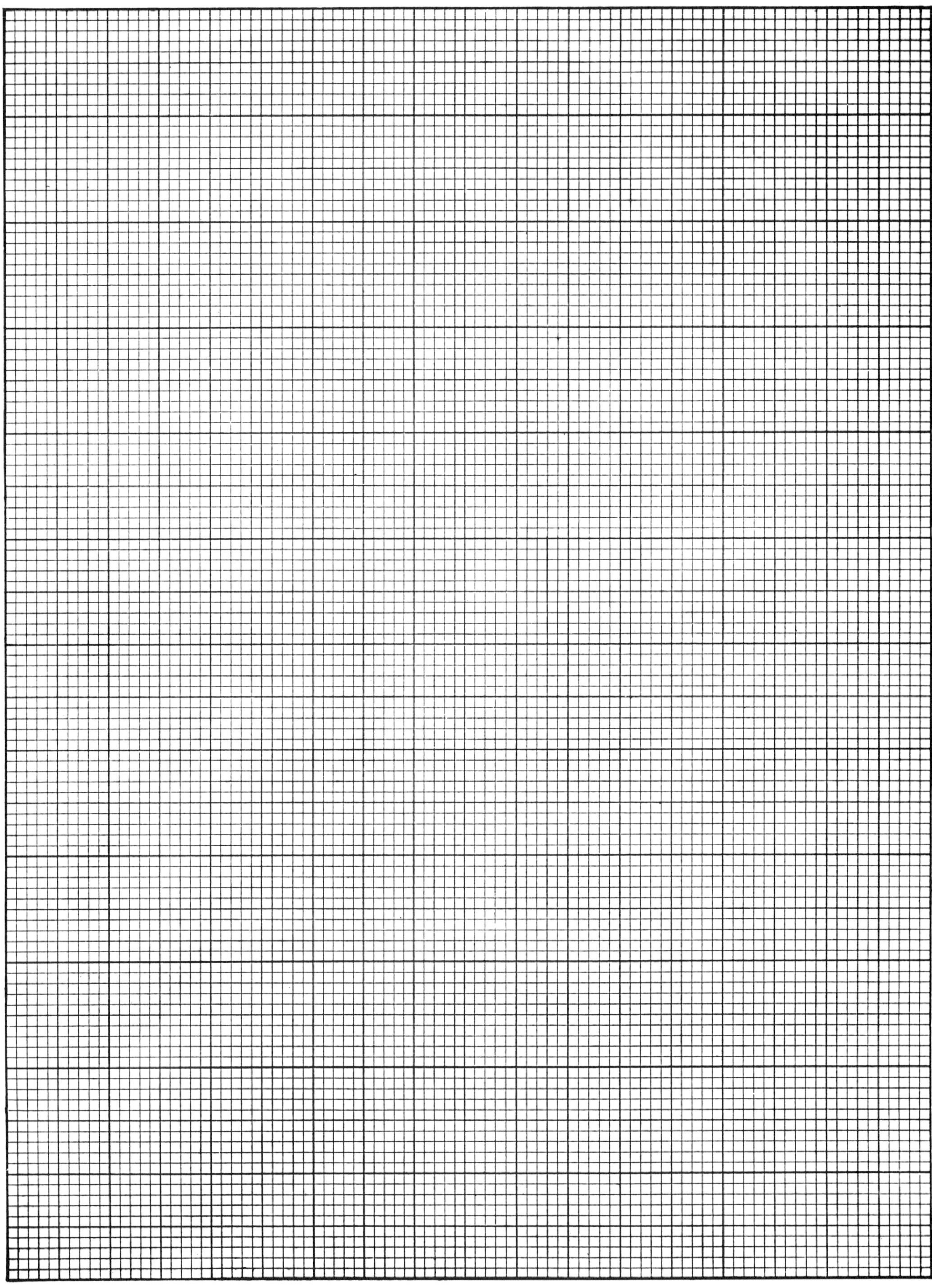

Data Sheet

t_1

t_2

$t_2 - t_1$

S_N

P_N

a_N

ω_N

t_I

λ_t

Date of Opposition

α_N

δ_N

Experiment 5

The Distance Between the Earth and Sun

I. Introduction

One of the most important units of distance in astronomy is the mean distance between the Earth and the Sun, or the so-called astronomical unit (AU). The astronomical unit is most often used to express interplanetary distances as well as orbital dimensions of distant binary star systems. Moreover, the trigonometric parallaxes used to determine the distances to stars employ as a base line this same unit of distance. Thus, a determination of the astronomical unit in terms of a unit of length that is well defined here on the earth such as the mile or the kilometer is of considerable value to the astronomer. To make such a determination, the distance to an object must be measured simultaneously but independently in miles or kilometers and in AU's. In this exercise you will obtain the size of the astronomical unit based on observations made of a transit of the planet Mercury which occurred on May 10, 1970.

II. Measurements

Remove Figures 5.1 and 5.2 from your text and superimpose the two photographs so that the background sunspot groups coincide. With these photographs so aligned, determine the center to center shift x_p of the disk of the planet Mercury (circular spot) relative to the background sunspots. Measure also the length x_o of the 12 arcsecond scaling line. Enter all of your results in your data

FIGURE 5.1

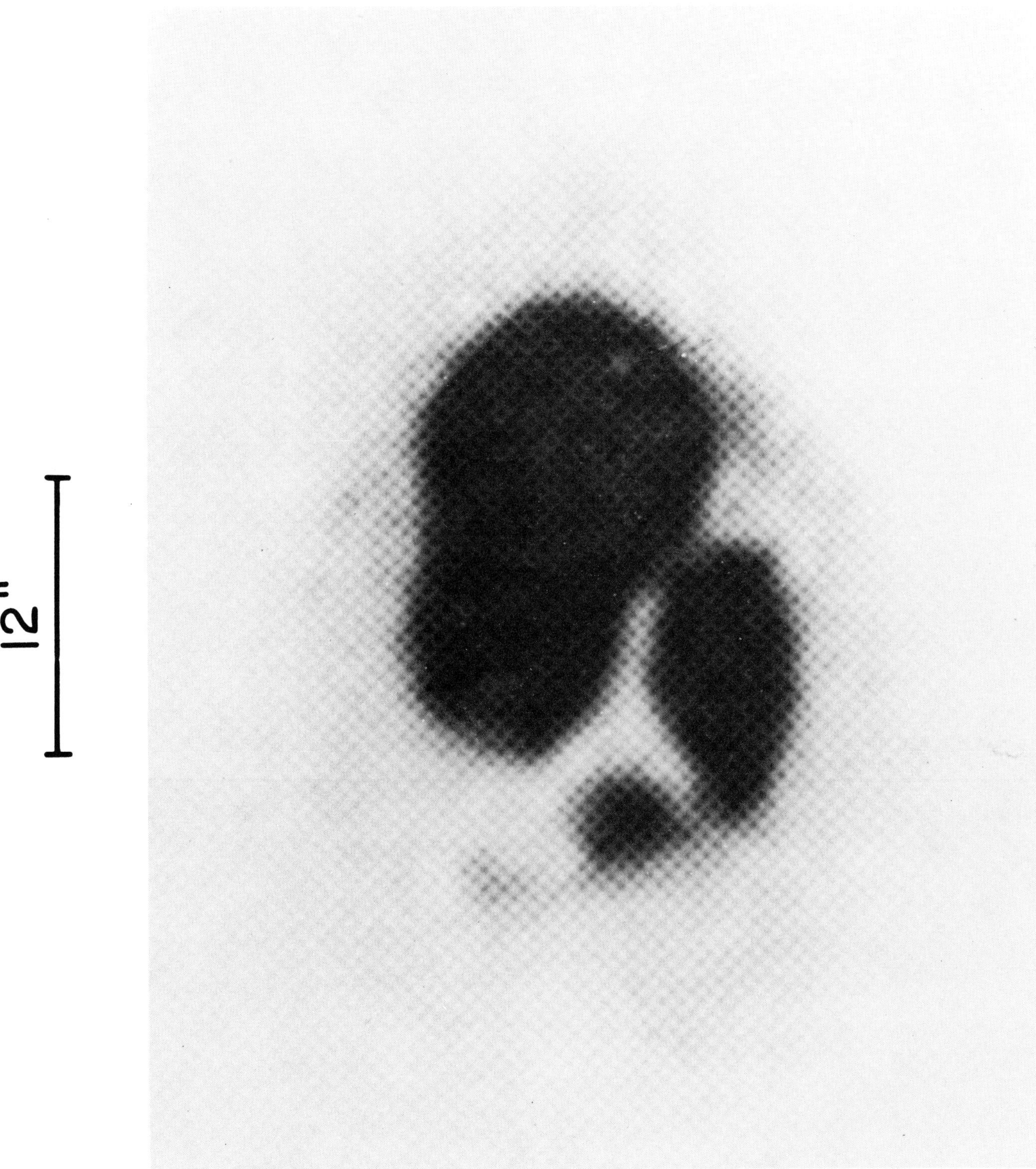

FIGURE 5.2

sheet. The remainder of the data necessary for this experiment are listed in Table 5.1 in which the angular separations ρ between Mercury and the Sun before and after the transit are presented along with their respective dates.

Table 5.1

The Positions of Mercury and the Sun

Date		Separation ρ
April	4	11.9°
	11	18.2
	18	20.1
	25	18.5
May	2	11.0
	9 (Transit)	0.0
	16	10.9
	23	19.5
	30	24.2
June	5	25.6
	12	24.1
	19	20.4

III. Reductions

On a sheet of graph paper, plot ρ versus the time t and determine the maximum values of ρ before and after the transit, ρ_{maxb} and ρ_{maxa}. The distances in astronomical units between Mercury and the Sun at greatest eastern and western elongation are given by

$$(5.1) \quad \begin{aligned} d_e(AU) &= \sin(\rho_{maxb}) \\ d_w(AU) &= \sin(\rho'_{maxa}) \end{aligned}$$

After computing d_e and d_w, plot these values versus the time corresponding to ρ_{maxb} and ρ_{maxa}. These times can be read off the ρ versus t plot from above. Connect the two resulting points with a straight line and read off the value d_o of the Mercury-Sun distance at the time of transit. The distance d_{EM} between the Earth and Mercury in AU at the time of the transit is then

$$(5.2) \quad d_{EM}(AU) = 1.00 - d_o$$

Calculate $d_{EM}(AU)$ and enter your result in your data sheet.

Assuming that s is the base line separation between the observing sites at Varberg, Sweden, and Yaounde, Cameroon, the distance $d_{EM}(km)$ between the Earth and Mercury in kilometers is then

$$(5.3) \quad d_{EM}(km) = \frac{206265}{12} \frac{sx_o}{x_p}$$

where the value of s is equal to 5100 kilometers. The number of kilometers N in an AU is then

$$(5.5) \quad N(km/AU) = \frac{d_{EM}(km)}{d_{EM}(AU)}$$

Calculate $d_{EM}(km)$ and N and enter your results in your data sheet.

IV. Questions

1. Show by means of diagrams why Mercury's angular separation from the sun passes through a maximum value.

2. The mass of the sun in grams can be calculated from Kepler's Harmonic Law $M_{\odot} = 4\pi^2 a^3/GP^2$ where a is the earth-sun distance in cm, P is the earth's sidereal period in seconds, and G is the universal gravitational constant in CGS units. Convert your N value into centimeters and compute $M_{\odot}$ in grams, recalling that $P = 3.16 \times 10^7$ sec and G is 6.67×10^{-8} dyne-cm^2/gm^2. How does this compare with the mass of the earth which is equal to about 6×10^{27} grams?

3. Would observations of a transit of the sun by the planet Venus yield more accurate results? Explain.

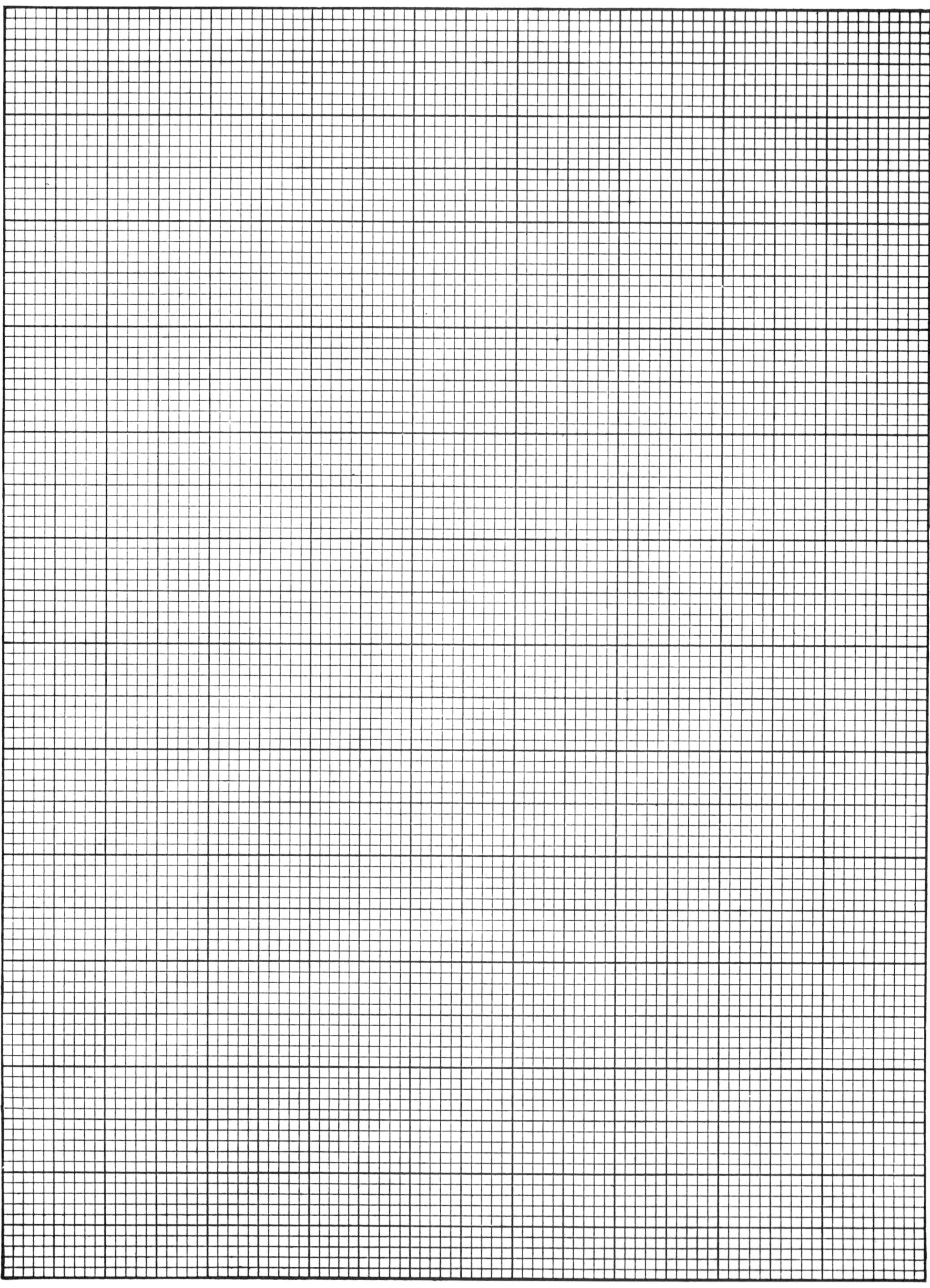

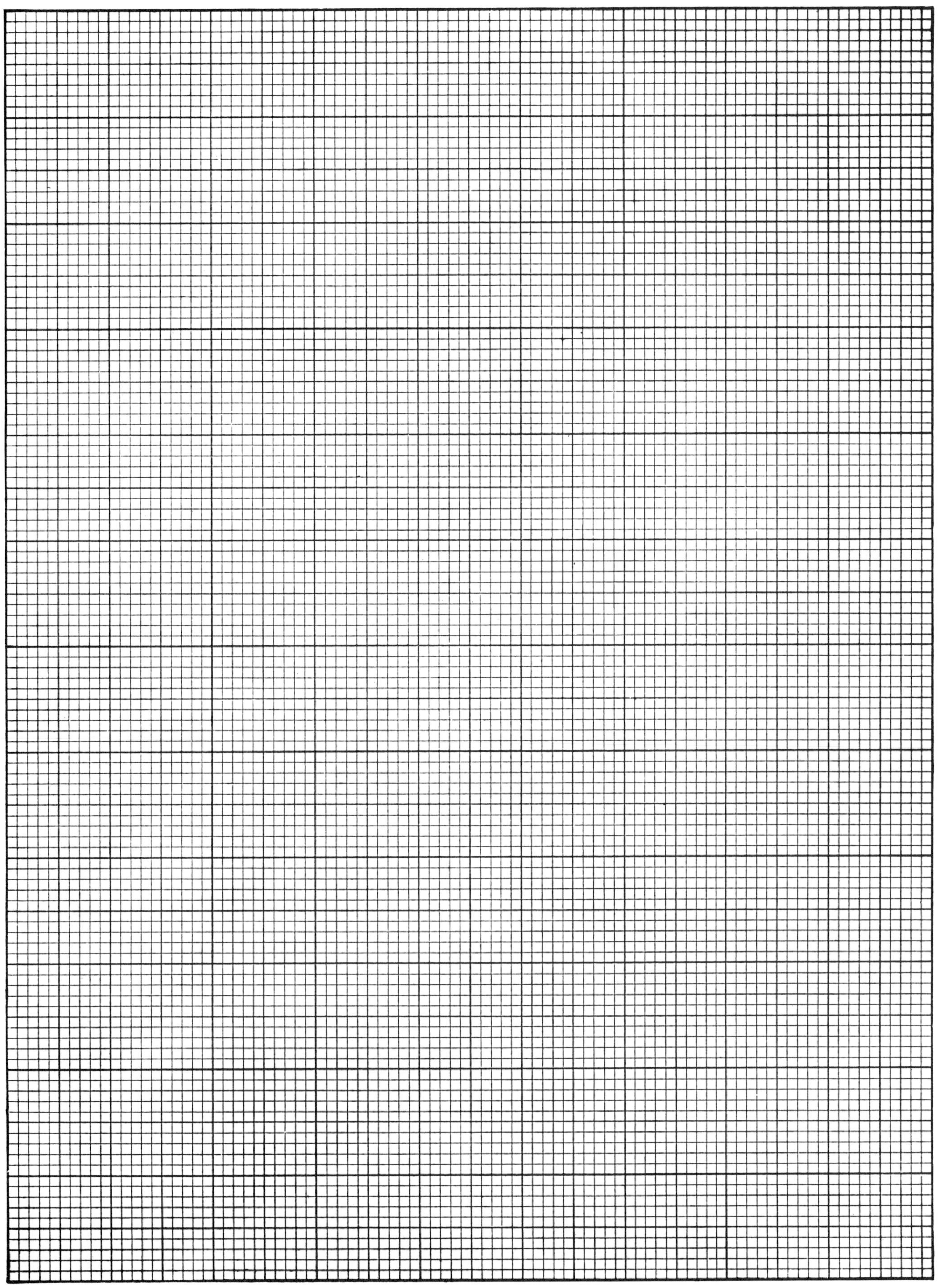

Data Sheet

ρ_{maxb}

$\sin(\rho_{maxb})$

d_e

ρ_{maxa}

$\sin(\rho_{maxa})$

d_w

d_o

d_{EM}(AU)

x_p

x_o

d_{EM}(km)

N (km/AU)

Experiment 6

Observations of an Artificial Satellite

I. Introduction

With the launch of the first artificial satellite in 1957, geophysicists were given a highly useful tool for probing the gravitational properties of the earth. In this exercise, you will make use of a pair of photographic observations of an artificial satellite to determine the mass of the earth.

II. Measurements

The basic measurements for this exercise will be made from Figures 6.1 and 6.2 in which an artificial satellite has been simultaneously photographed from two separate locations 228 km apart. Also, during both exposures, the camera lenses were alternately covered and uncovered in tandem at four second intervals.

Remove Figures 6.1 and 6.2 from your text and superimpose the two photographs so that the background star patterns coincide. With the photographs so aligned, measure the distance x_s between the midpoints of the middle segments of the two satellite trails. Measure the lengths of each one of the satellite trail dashes and find the mean length x_d of the trail segments. Measure the length x_o of the 10° scaling line. Take care to measure x_s, x_d, and x_o in the same units. Enter your results in your data sheet.

III. Reductions

Calculate the parallax p of the satellite as viewed from the two different locations where p is given by

$$(6.1) \quad p = 10.0°\{x_s/x_o\}$$

If the satellite-observer configuration is that shown in Figure 6.3, then the altitude h of the satellite is

$$(6.2) \quad h = \frac{d_o}{2\tan(p/2)}$$

The semi-major axis a of the orbit of the satellite is then equal to $h + R_\oplus$ where $R_\oplus$ is the earth's radius. Calculate h, using equation (6.2), assuming a value of d_o equal to 228 kilometers and $R_\oplus$ equal to 6370 kilometers. Calculate the corresponding value for the radius a of the satellite orbit and enter your values of p, h, and a in your data sheet.

The linear distance d_s that the satellite moves in a four-second interval is the linear distance of each trail segment of the satellite and is given by

$$(6.3) \quad d_s = \frac{\alpha_d h}{206265}$$

where α_d in arcseconds is $3.6 \times 10^4 \{x_d/x_o\}$. The corresponding satellite velocity v_s is simply d_s/t_s, where $t_s = 4.0$ sec. The sidereal period P_s of the satellite is then

FIGURE 6.1

FIGURE 6.2

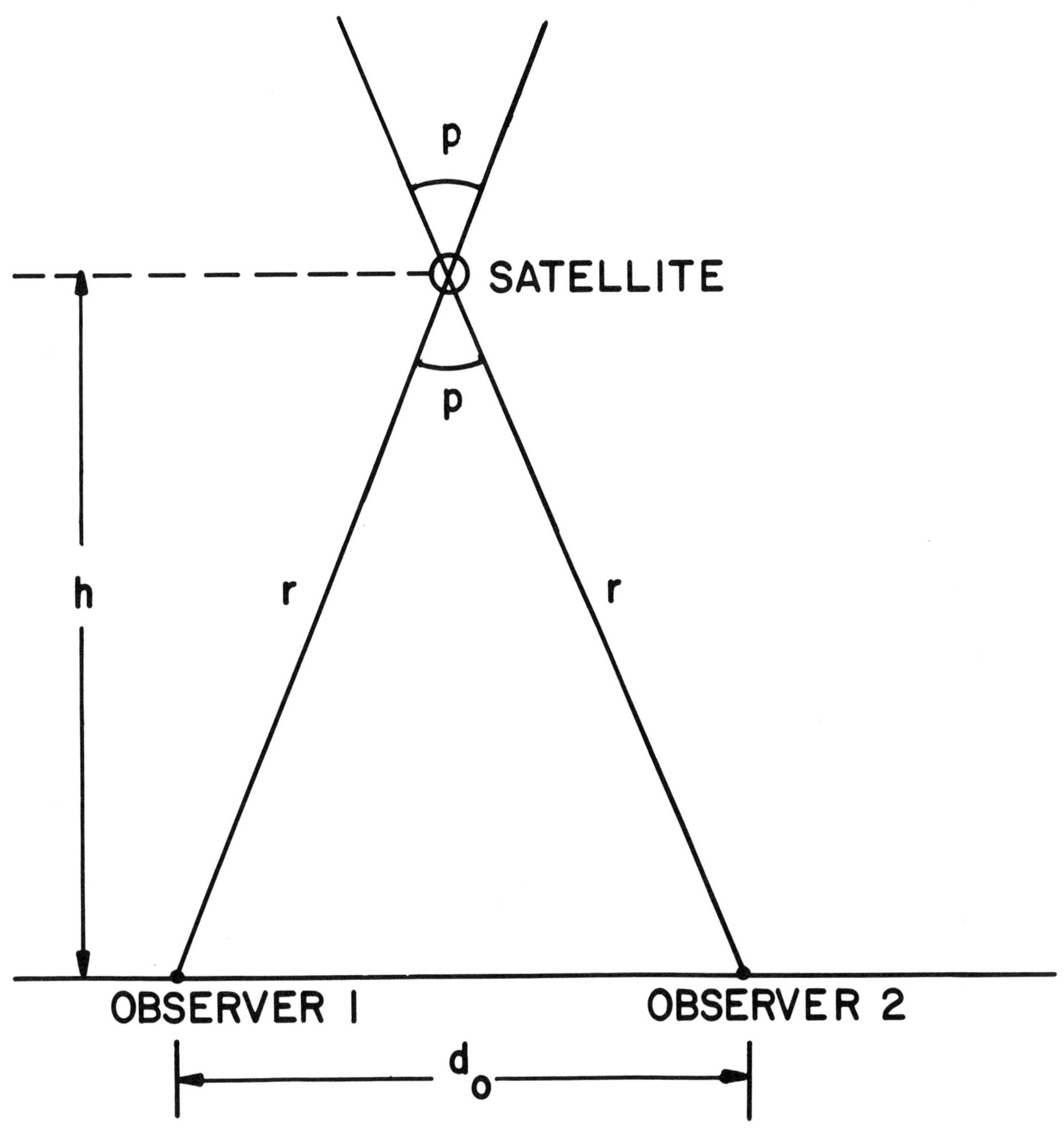

FIGURE 6.3

$$(6.4) \quad P_s = \frac{2\pi a}{v_s}$$

Compute d_s, v_s, and P_s for the satellite, and, using these values, calculate the mass of the earth $M_\oplus$ from Kepler's Harmonic Law;

$$(6.5) \quad M_\oplus = \frac{4\pi^2 a^3}{G\,P_s^2}$$

where G is the universal constant of gravitation.

IV. Questions

1. If the camera lenses were alternately covered and uncovered in four second intervals during the exposures shown in Figures 6.1 and 6.2, discuss why the satellite images came out in the form of dashed lines.

2. Discuss the assumptions that have been made in this exercise.

3. Compute the mean density of the earth, assuming that the earth is in the shape of a sphere. If the mean surface density of the earth is about 3.3 grams/cm^3, what can be deduced about the nature of the earth's interior?

Data Sheet

x_o

x_s

x_d

d_o

p

tan(p/2)

h

a

α_d

d_s

v_s

P_s

$M_{\oplus}$

Experiment 7

The Atmospheres of Venus and Mars

I. Introduction

A detailed analysis of planetary atmospheres generally requires spectroscopic methods and equipment that are beyond the scope of an elementary astronomy course. Two of the terrestrial planets, Venus and Mars, however, both possess atmospheres which lend themselves to partial investigation by non-spectroscopic methods. In this exercise you will perform one such simple analysis.

II. Measurements

Measure the diameter d_c of the inner border of the refraction ring of the image of Venus shown in Figure 7.1 as well as the thickness t of the refraction ring. Both d_c and t should be measured along several diameters of Venus and the results averaged. Measure also the diameters of the ultraviolet and infrared images of Mars shown in Figure 7.2 across several diameters and average your results to obtain d_{IR} and d_{UV}, the infrared and ultraviolet diameters of Mars. Enter all of your results in your data sheet.

III. Reductions

Calculate the approximate depth h_V of the atmosphere of Venus using the relationship

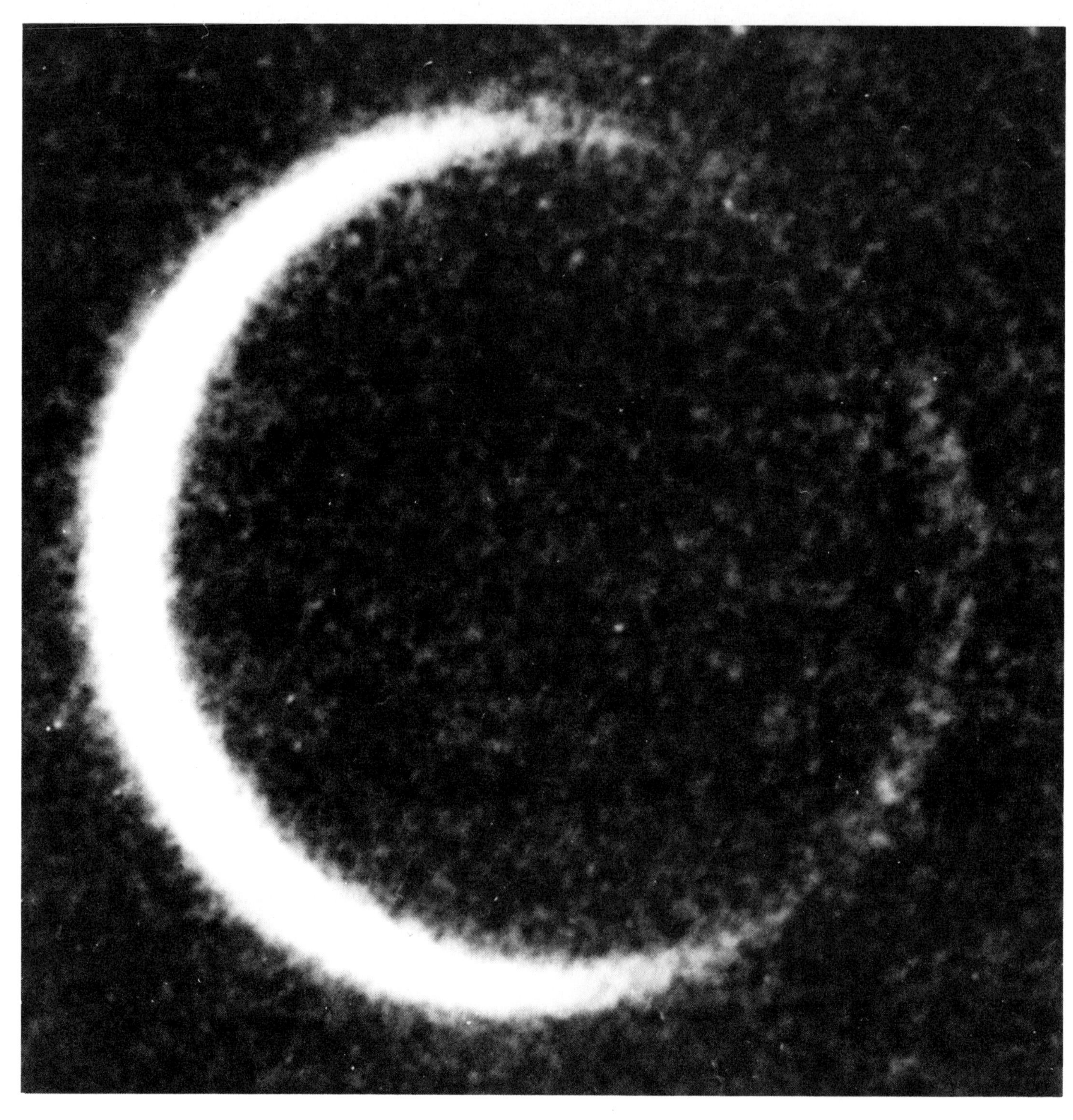

FIGURE 7.1

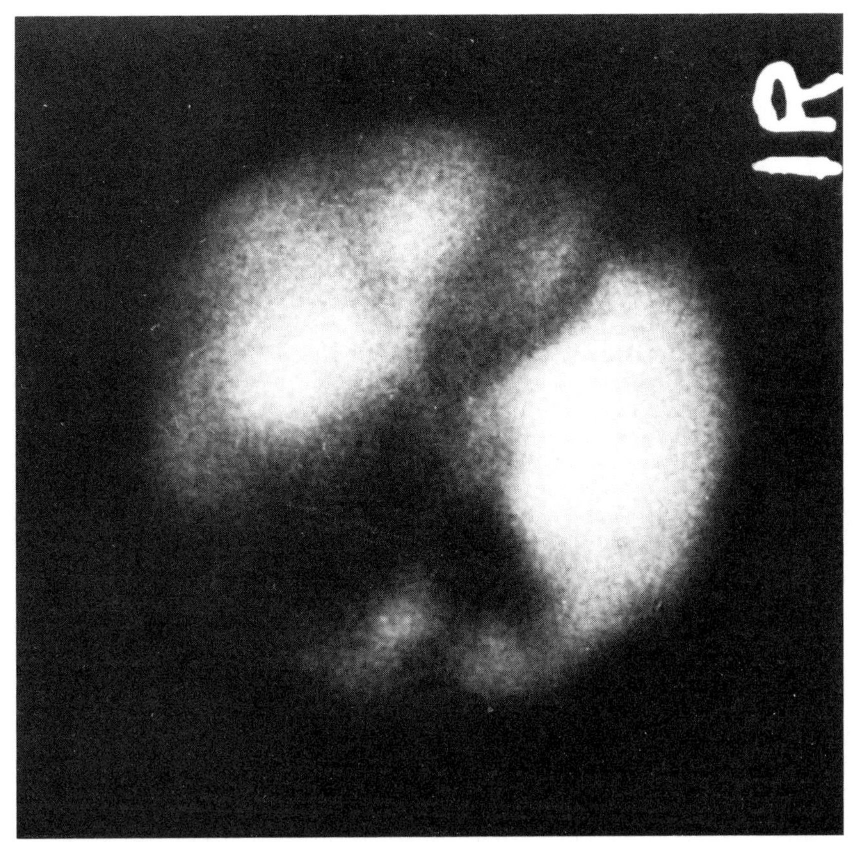

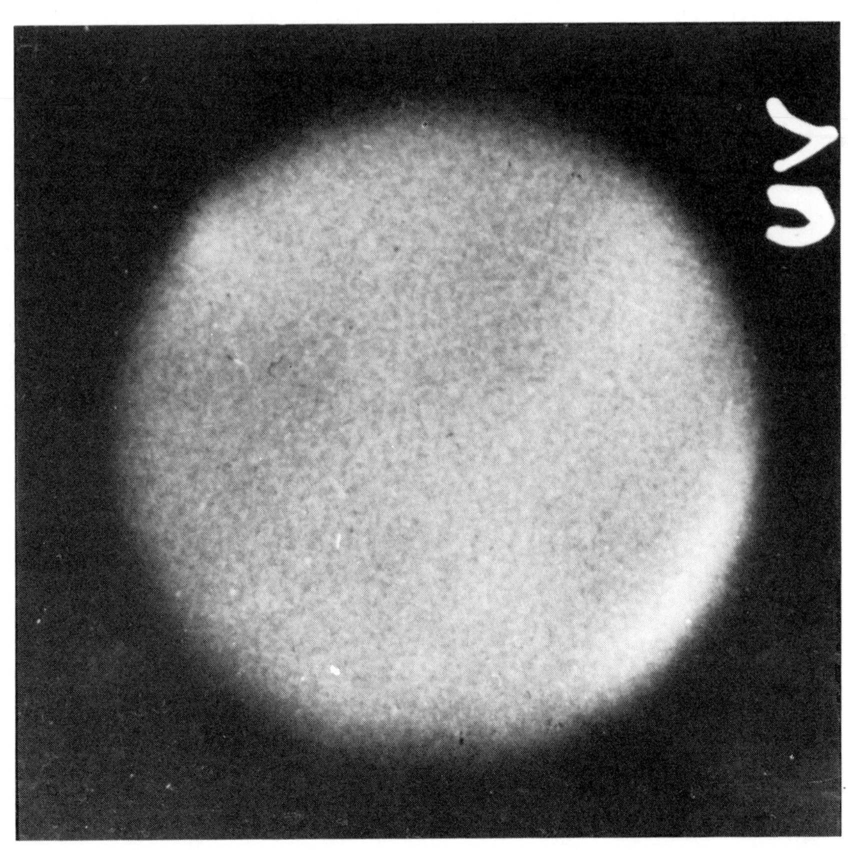

FIGURE 7.2

$$(7.1) \quad h_v = \frac{tD_v}{d_c}$$

The quantity D_v is the true linear diameter of Venus' surface and is equal to 12,200 km. For the planet Mars, the atmospheric thickness h_m is given by

$$(7.2) \quad h_m = \frac{D_m(d_{UV} - d_{IR})}{2\ d_{IR}}$$

where D_m is the true linear diameter of Mars' surface and is equal to 6550 km. Calculate the atmospheric thicknesses in centimeters for both Venus and Mars and enter your results in your data sheet. The scale height H is defined as the height at which the pressure P(r) is 1/e or 1/2.72 times the surface pressure. As an approximation assume that the scale height is roughly equal to h/30 and calculate the scale heights for the atmospheres of Venus and Mars in cm. Enter your results in your data sheet.

The mean molecular weight $\bar{\mu}$ of an ideal planetary atmosphere is related to the scale height of the atmosphere by

$$(7.3) \quad \bar{\mu} = \frac{kT}{H\ m_H\ g}$$

Using this relation, compute the mean molecular weights of the atmospheres of Venus and Mars, assuming the values for the surface gravity g and the mean temperature T of Venus and Mars are those listed in Table 7.1. The quantity m_H is the mass of the hydrogen atom and is equal to 1.67×10^{-24} grams. Also estimate the uncertainties in your value for $\bar{\mu}$.

Table 7.1

Planet	Mean Temperature	Surface Gravity
Venus	600°K	880 cm/sec^2
Mars	270°K	390 cm/sec^2

IV. Questions

1. Explain the ring of light exhibited by the planet Venus in Figure 7.1.

2. Why is the size of the infrared image of Mars the same as the actual linear diameter of Mars' surface while the size of the ultraviolet image is equal to the solid surface diameter plus twice the depth of the Martian atmosphere?

3. Spectroscopic analysis of both the atmospheres of Venus and Mars indicate that the principal constituent is carbon dioxide ($\mu = 44$). Is this result consistent with your findings? What other substances might be present based on <u>your</u> results?

Data Sheet

Venus

d_c

t

h_v

H_v

$\bar{\mu}_v$

Mars

d_{IR}

d_{UV}

h_m

H_m

$\bar{\mu}_m$

Experiment 8

The Mass of Jupiter

I. Introduction

Over half of the planets in the solar system possess one or more natural satellites. As in the case of artificial satellites, studies of the motions of these natural satellites can yield a great deal of interesting and useful information concerning the gravitational properties of the primary planet. In the exercise that follows, a series of photographs of Jupiter's Galilean satellites are presented from which you will obtain the mass of the planet Jupiter itself.

II. Measurements

Using Figures 8.1 to 8.4, measure the center to center distance r between the images of Jupiter and Satellite I as accurately as possible for all eight photographs in the set. Measure also the length x_o of the 4 arcminute calibration line. Repeat the measurements for Satellites II, III, and IV. Enter your results in your data sheet.

III. Reductions

Having completed the measurements of r, plot the resulting values versus the total elapsed time using the observation times in Universal Time listed below each photograph. Pass a smooth curve through the resulting points and determine the maximum value r_o of the satellite distance from Jupiter. Choose two points on this curve, one on each side of the maximum point, which are near but not beyond the end points of the plot. If r_1 and r_2 are the satellite distances of the selected points, then from Figure 8.5 it can be seen that the angles θ_1 and θ_2 traversed by the satellite to (or from) its greatest elongation point are simply given by

$$(8.1) \qquad \begin{aligned} \cos\theta_1 &= r_1/r_o \\ \cos\theta_2 &= r_2/r_o \end{aligned}$$

The values of $\cos\theta_1$ and $\cos\theta_2$ for your chosen points should be calculated along with the corresponding values for θ_1 and θ_2. It should be possible to find your θ values to the nearest degree. The total angle $\Delta\theta$ traversed by the satellite in moving from point 1 to point 2 is then equal to $\theta_1 + \theta_2$ and should be calculated for your data. From your plot of r versus t, determine the value of Δt, the time for the satellite to move from point 1 to point 2. For a circular orbit, the sidereal period P is then given by

$$(8.2) \qquad P = 360°\{\Delta t/\Delta\theta\}$$

where the units of P are the same as those of the quantity Δt. Calculate the sidereal period for Satellite I using Equation (8.2), and convert the resulting value into years. Repeat the above procedure in its entirety to obtain the sidereal periods of Satellites II, III, and IV. Enter all of your results in your data sheet.

Determine the linear radius a of each of the satellite orbits using the relation

$$(8.3) \qquad a = \frac{240\ r_o D}{206265\ x_o}$$

where D is the distance between Jupiter and the earth. For the photographs shown in Figures 8.1 to 8.4, you may assume that the value of D is 4.46 AU. Since the orbits of all of the Galilean satellites are nearly circular, the value of a so determined represents the mean distance between Jupiter and the satellite. Calculate the value of a for each of the four Galilean satellites and enter your results in your data sheet.

Construct a graph of a^3 versus P^2 for your satellite data using the ordinate as your a^3-axis and the abscissa as your P^2-axis. Kepler's Harmonic Law states that the squares of the sidereal periods of the planets are in direct proportion to the cubes of their mean distances from the sun. Thus, a plot of a^3 versus P^2 for a given system should yield a straight line if the system obeys the Harmonic Law. Verify from your a^3 versus P^2 plot that Jupiter's Galilean satellites do indeed obey the Harmonic Law.

From Newtonian mechanics it can be shown that the ratio a^3/P^2 for a two-body problem is equal to $(M_1 + M_2)G/4\pi^2$ where M_1 and M_2 are the masses of the bodies involved and G is the universal gravitational constant. For the Galilean satellites, the satellite mass M_S is negligible compared to the mass M_J of Jupiter and the ratio a^3/P^2 is then simply the product of the mass of Jupiter and $G/4\pi^2$. If a is measured in Au, P in years, and M_J in solar masses, then the value of $G/4\pi^2$ is one, and the mass of Jupiter is given by the slope of the a^3 versus P^2 plot. Find the mass of Jupiter in solar masses by determining the slope of the a^3 versus P^2 plot and enter your results in your data sheet.

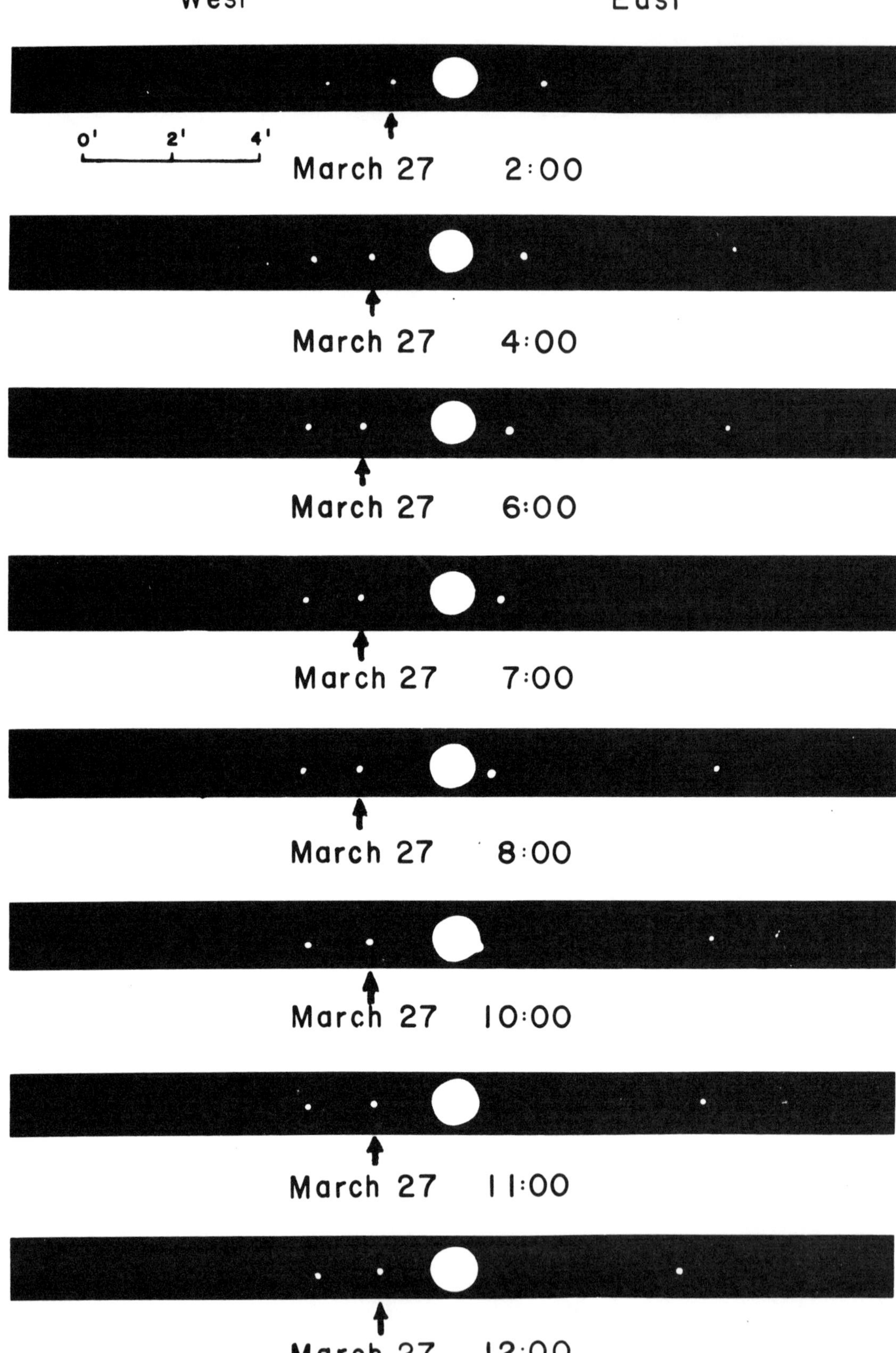
Satellite I
West
East
0'
2'
4'
March 27 2:00
March 27 4:00
March 27 6:00
March 27 7:00
March 27 8:00
March 27 10:00
March 27 11:00
March 27 12:00

FIGURE 8.1

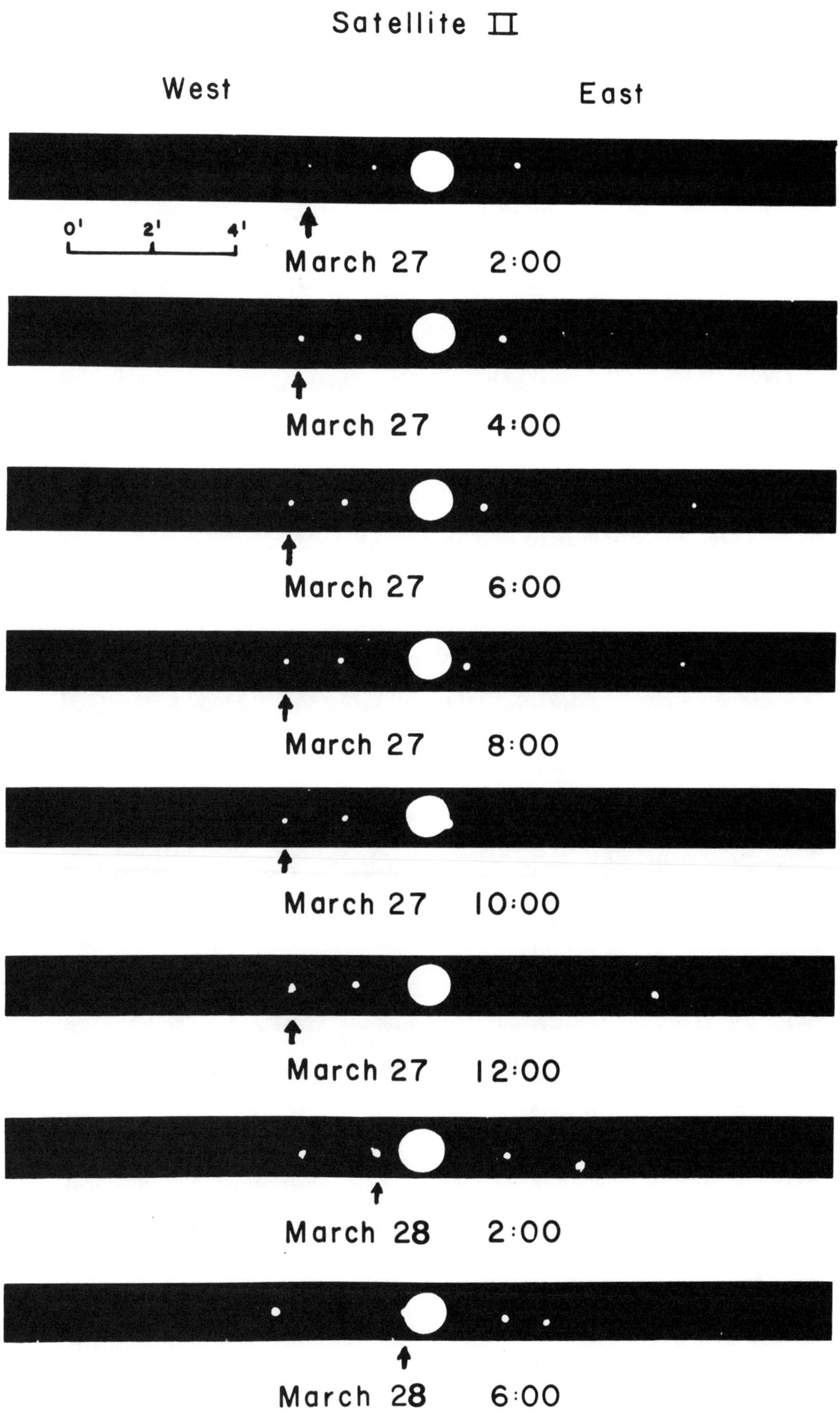

Satellite II

FIGURE 8.2

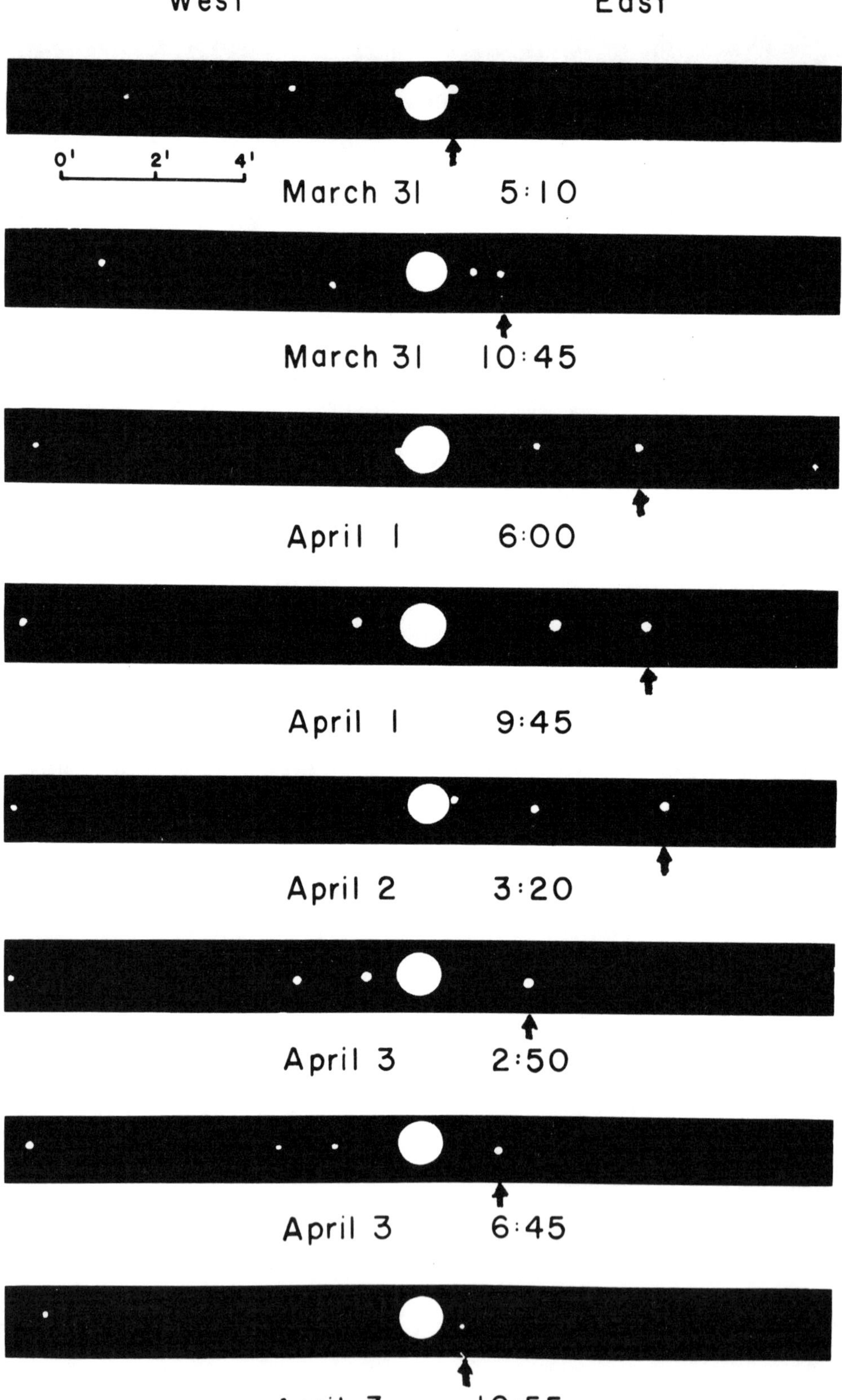
Satellite III
West
East
0'
2'
4'
March 31 5:10
March 31 10:45
April 1 6:00
April 1 9:45
April 2 3:20
April 3 2:50
April 3 6:45
April 3 10:55

FIGURE 8.3

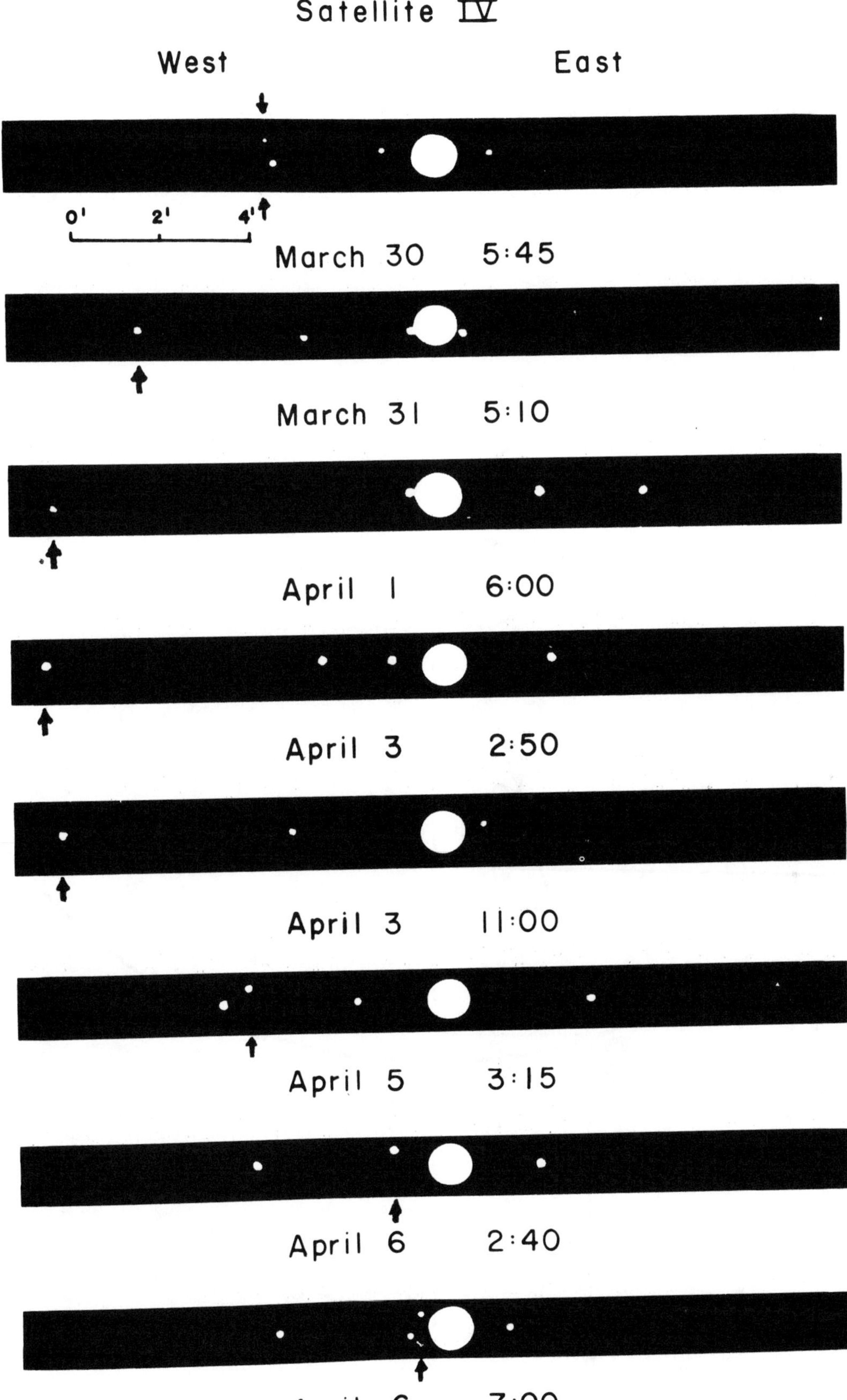
Satellite IV
West
East
0'
2'
4'
March 30 5:45
March 31 5:10
April 1 6:00
April 3 2:50
April 3 11:00
April 5 3:15
April 6 2:40
April 6 7:00

FIGURE 8.4

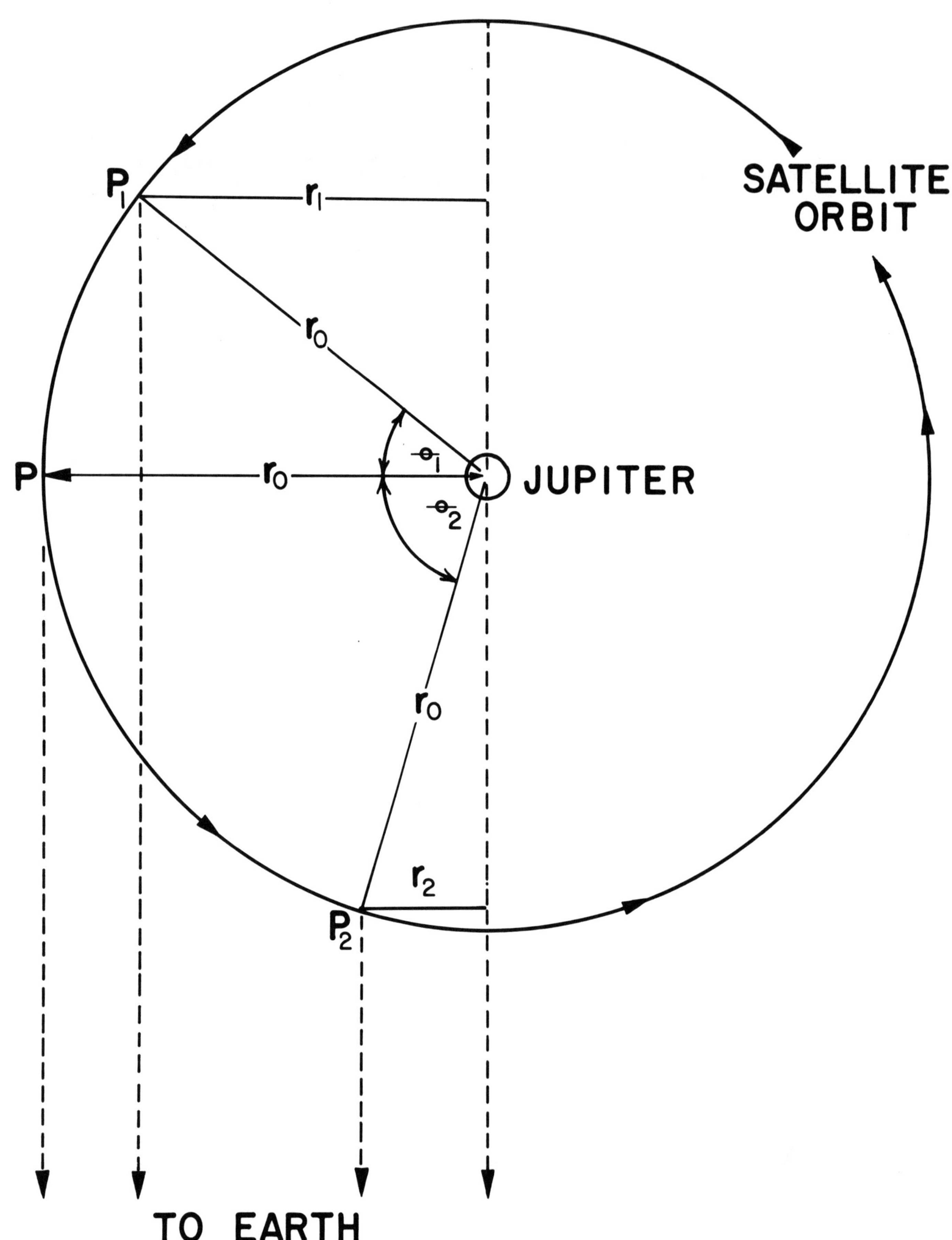

FIGURE 8.5

IV. Questions

1. Which of Kepler's laws of planetary motion have we assumed?

2. What additional assumptions have been made in this exercise?

3. The least massive stars known have masses of about 1/25 that of the sun. From your value of M_J, how much more massive does Jupiter need to be in order to dimly shine as a star?

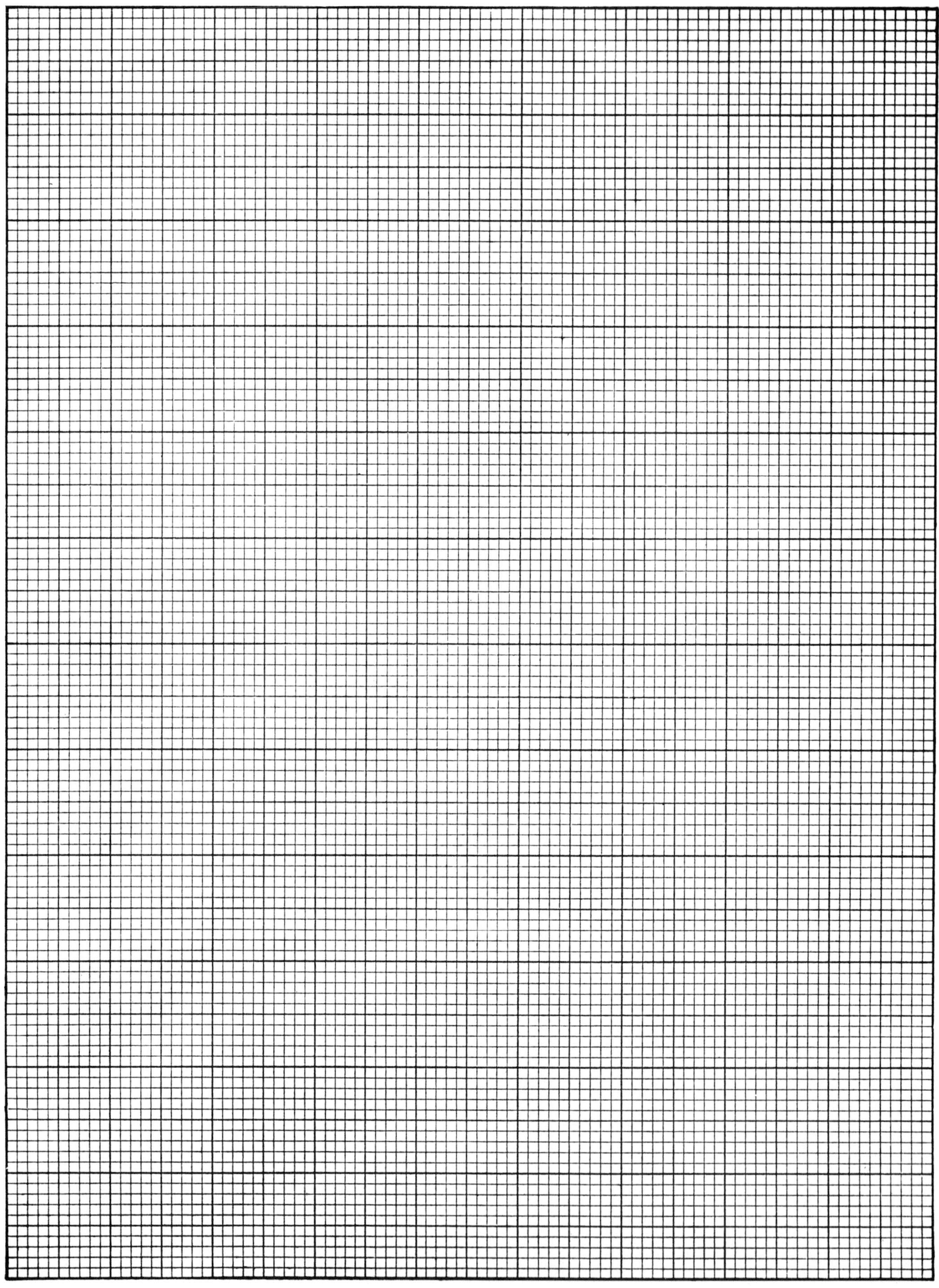

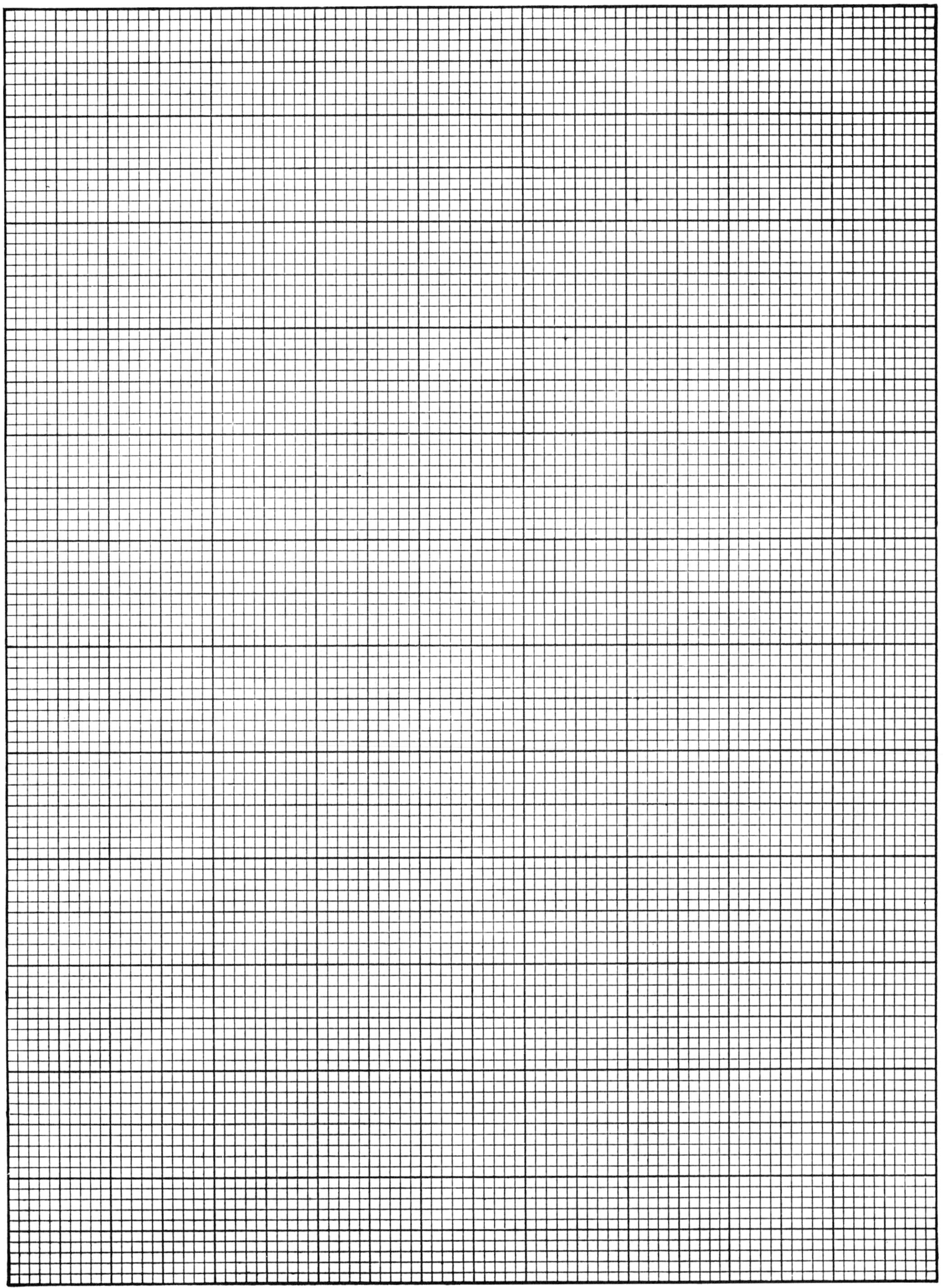

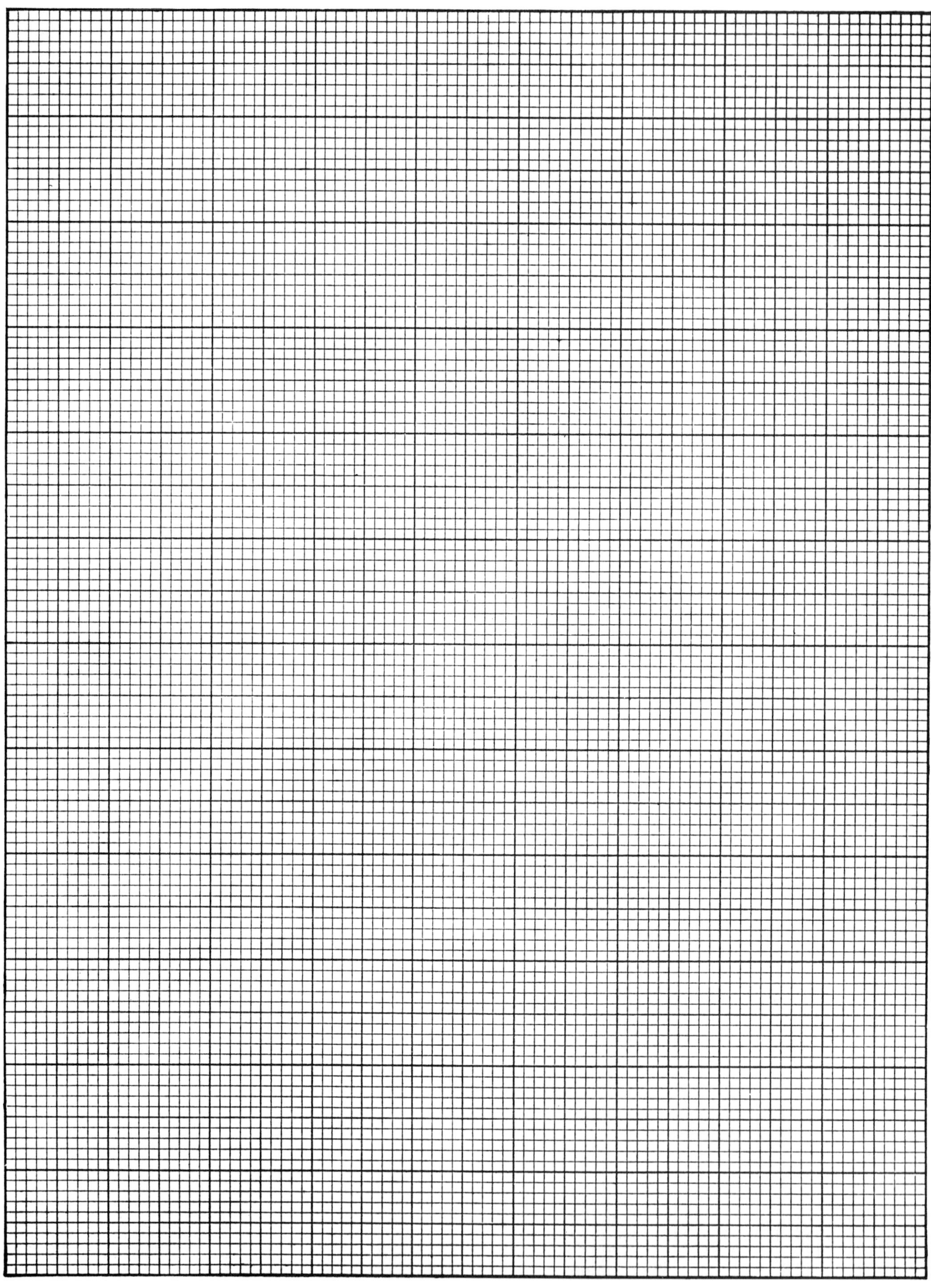

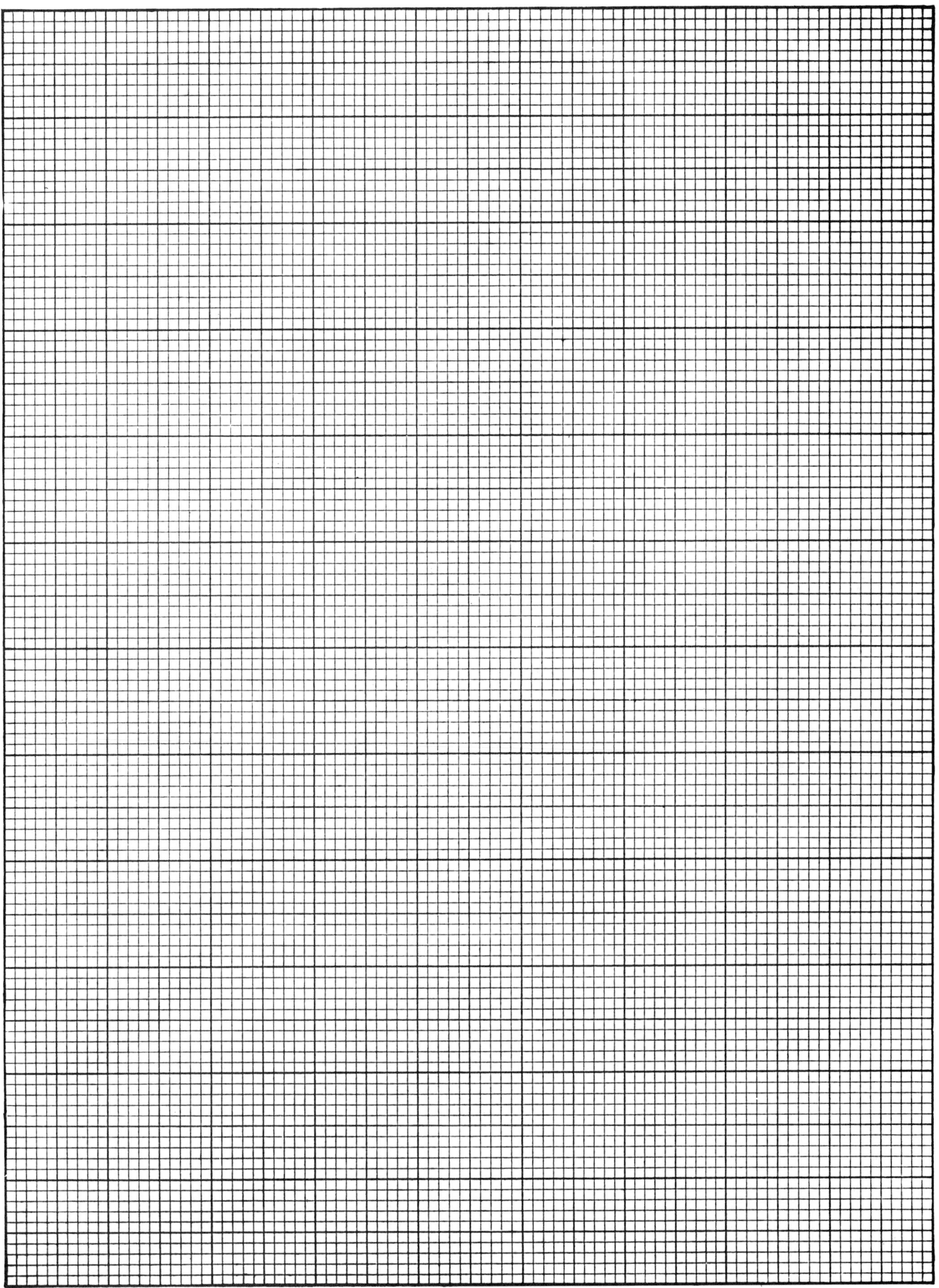

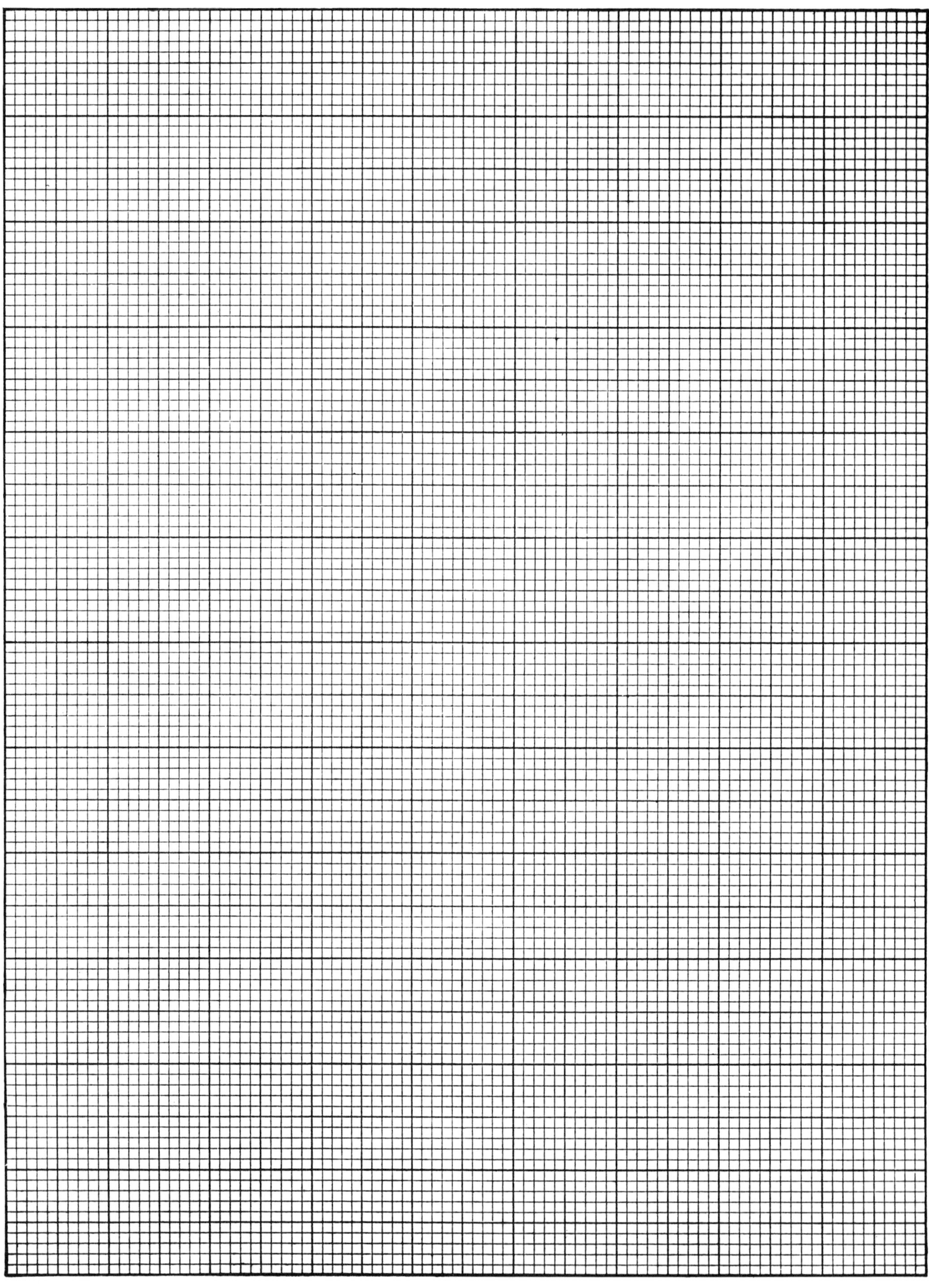

Data Sheet

Satellite	I		II		III		IV	
Image	t (hr)	r (mm)	t (hr)	r (mm)	t (hr)	r (mm)	t (hr)	r (mm)
1								
2								
3								
4								
5								
6								
7								
8								
r_o								
r_1								
r_2								
$\cos\theta_1$								
θ_1								
$\cos\theta_2$								
θ_2								
$\Delta\theta$								
Δt								
P								
P^2								
x_o								
r_o								
a								
a^3								
M_J								

Experiment 9

The Continuous Spectrum of the Sun

I. Introduction

The distribution of the solar energy by wavelength constitutes what is referred to by astronomers as the continuous spectrum of the sun or solar continuum. It is the purpose of this exercise to derive some of the sun's physical properties through a simple analysis of the solar continuum.

II. Procedure

Using the data from Table 9.1, plot the flux, f_λ, versus its corresponding wavelength on a sheet of graph paper and sketch a curve through <u>all</u> of the points. The curve should be very carefully done, since this plot will be the basis of this entire exercise.

III. Reductions

As accurately as possible determine from your plot the wavelength at which f_λ takes on its greatest value. This wavelength of maximum light λ_{max} can be related to the Kelvin temperature of the sun $T_\odot$ by Wien's Law

$$(9.1) \quad \lambda_{max} T = w$$

where the constant w has a value of 2.898×10^7 for λ_{max} in Å and T in Kelvin degrees. Using equation (9.1) and your measured value of λ_{max}, compute the value of the Wien's Law temperature T_w for the sun.

Table 9.1

The Continuous Spectrum of the Sun

λ (Å)	f_λ (ergs/cm^2/Å/sec)	λ (Å)	f_λ (ergs/cm^2/Å/sec)
2000	1.2	4600	215
2200	4.5	4800	213
2400	6.4	5000	204
2600	13	5500	198
2800	25	6000	187
3000	59	6500	167
3200	85	7000	149
3400	114	7500	129
3600	115	8000	114
3700	127	9000	90
3800	121	10000	74
3900	115	11000	61
4000	160	12000	50
4100	187	14000	33
4200	189	16000	22
4300	183	18000	15
4400	201	20000	10
4500	213	25000	5.0

Find the total area A under the f_λ versus λ plot. This can be accomplished by the use of a planimeter, by simple numerical integration (Trapezoidal Rule, Simpson's Rule, etc.), or even by simple square counts. Your instructor will indicate the method to be employed. Once you have determined the area, convert the result into ergs/cm^2/sec. The conversion factor will be determined by the scale used on each axis for the original plot. This converted area, E_T, is equal to the total energy at all wavelengths striking one square centimeter of surface just outside of the earth's atmosphere and is referred to in astronomy as the solar constant. Compute your value for the solar constant and enter your result in your data sheet.

It is now necessary to calculate the total energy per unit area at the surface of the sun, $E_\odot$. This quantity is given simply by

$$(9.2) \quad E_\odot = E_T\{a^2/R_\odot{}^2\}$$

where a is the earth-sun distance and $R_\odot$ is the solar radius. The solar effective temperature T_e is given by Stefan's Law

$$(9.3) \quad E_\odot = \sigma T_e{}^4$$

The constant σ is the Stefan's constant and is equal to 5.669×10^{-5} in CGS units. Using Equation (9.3), calculate T_e for the sun and enter your result in your data sheet.

The luminosity or total energy output per unit time of the sun $L_\odot$ is simply the product of $E_\odot$ and the total surface area of the sun or

$$(9.4) \quad L_\odot = 4\pi R_\odot{}^2 E_\odot$$

Calculate the solar luminosity in ergs/sec and enter your result in your data sheet.

IV. Questions

1. The value for the flux listed in Table 9.1 are for outside of the earth's atmosphere. Which of these values will be most affected by the earth's atmosphere? Which will be least affected? Explain.

2. In what respects does the flux versus wavelength plot resemble a black-body curve? How is it different? Explain.

3. It is estimated that the earth's technology over the next several decades will require roughly 2×10^{28} ergs of energy/year to maintain itself. From your computed value of the solar energy output, could solar energy provide a reasonable source of energy to meet this "energy crisis"?

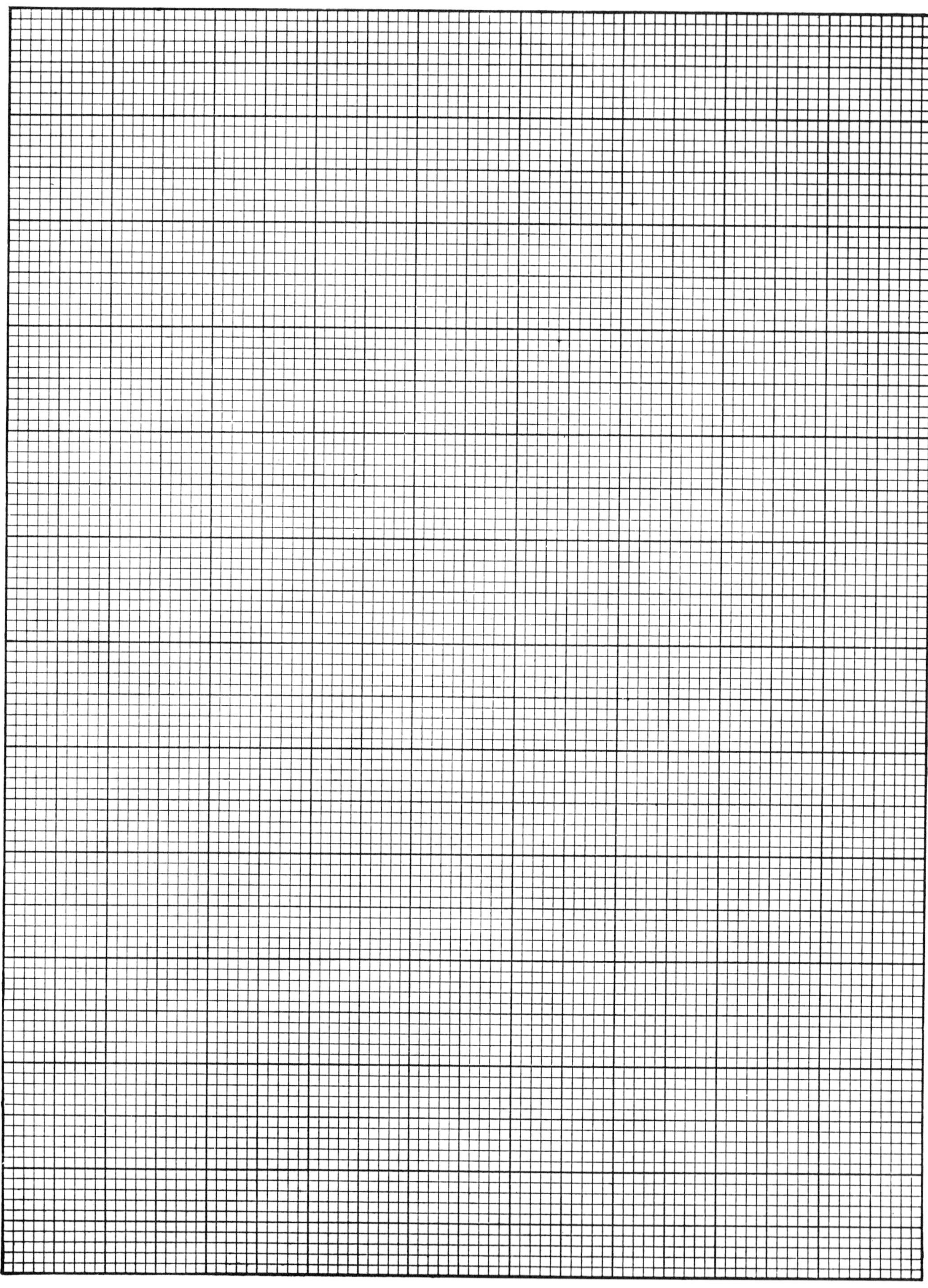

Data Sheet

λ_{max}

T_w

A

E_T

E_Θ

T_e

L_Θ

Experiment 10

The Space Motion of Barnard's Star

I. Introduction

Although one commonly refers to the distant stars as "fixed", all of them have motions of their own, which betray themselves both spectroscopically and astrometrically. In this exercise, you will investigate the motion of Barnard's Star, an object which is relatively near the sun and possesses substantial movement.

II. Measurements

The photograph shown in Figure 10.1 is a superposition of three plates taken of Barnard's Star at roughly six-month intervals. On the photograph draw a center-to-center line between the two lower images and measure its length d_μ. Measure also the perpendicular distance d_p between the center of the third image and your initial center-to-center line. In the same units, determine the length d_o of the 10 arcsecond scaling line at the bottom of Figure 10.1.

On the spectrogram shown in Figure 10.2, measure the distance x_o between the two comparison lines indicated. Also measure the distance x_{line} between the shortward comparison line and the 4415.13 Å stellar absorption line (see Appendix 7). Enter all of your results in your data sheet.

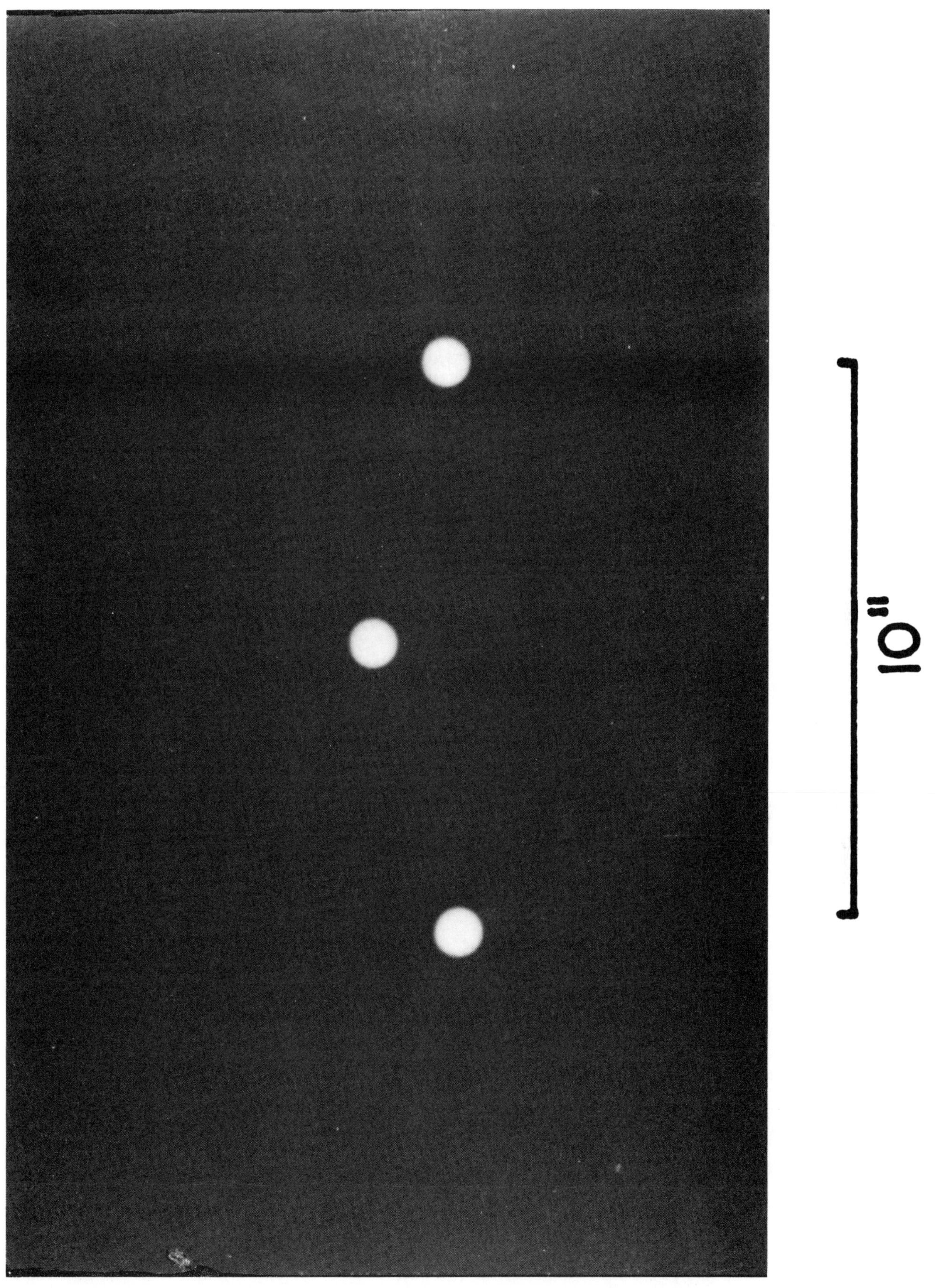

FIGURE 10.1

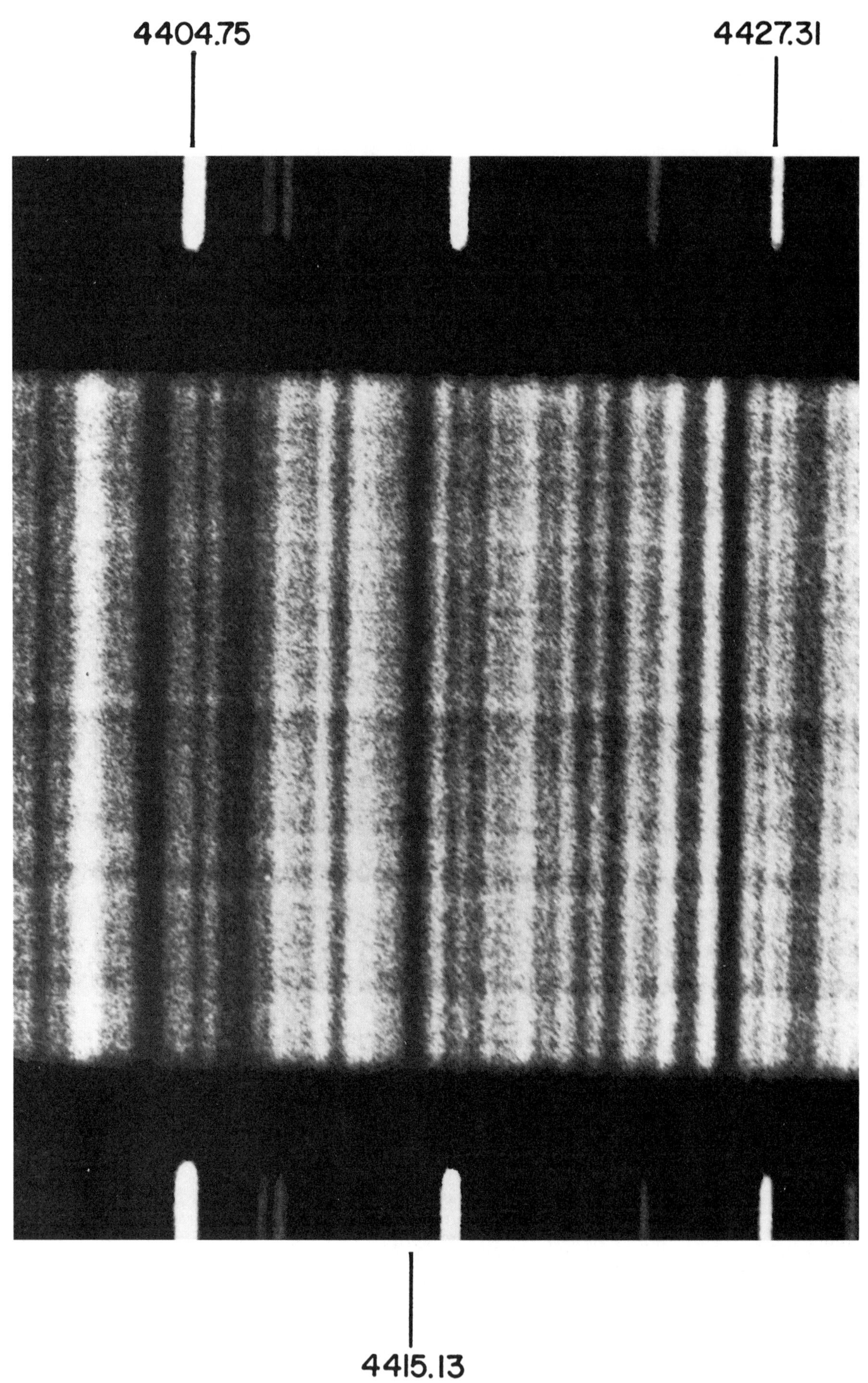

FIGURE 10.2

III. Reductions

Calculate the wavelength λ_{obs} of the indicated stellar absorption line using the relation

$$(10.1) \quad \lambda_{obs} = \lambda_1 + \frac{(\lambda_2 - \lambda_1)}{x_o} x_{line}$$

where λ_1 and λ_2 are the wavelengths of the two comparison lines. The Doppler shift is then defined as $(\lambda_{obs} - \lambda_{lab})/\lambda_{lab}$, where λ_{lab} is the laboratory wavelength of the designated feature. Find the value of the Doppler shift for Barnard's Star and enter your results in your data sheet. The component of velocity along the line of sight, or radial velocity V_r, is then

$$(10.2) \quad V_r = \frac{\lambda_{obs} - \lambda_{lab}}{\lambda_{lab}} c$$

where c is the velocity of light in km/sec.

The proper motion of Barnard's Star μ is given by

$$(10.3) \quad \mu = \frac{d_\mu}{d_o} 10''$$

Using this relation, calculate the proper motion of Barnard's Star in arcseconds/year and enter the result in your data sheet.

The parallax p of Barnard's Star is given by

$$(10.4) \quad p = \frac{d_p}{2d_o} 10''$$

whence the distance r in parsecs is

$$(10.5) \quad r = \frac{1}{p}$$

Calculate both p and r for Barnard's Star and enter your results in the data sheet.

The tangential velocity T or the component of velocity perpendicular to the line of sight can be written as

$$(10.6) \quad T = 4.74\ \mu\ r$$

if r is measured in parsecs and μ in arcseconds per year. The magnitude of the space velocity V of a star is the magnitude of the vector sum of its radial velocity V_r and its tangential velocity T, and can thus be written as

$$(10.7) \quad V = \sqrt{V_r^{\,2} + T^2}$$

Calculate both T and V and enter your results in your data sheet.

IV. Questions

1. Explain why a set of plates taken at times of 0, 6, and 12 months would produce the pattern of images of Barnard's Star shown in Figure 10.1 when the background stars of all three plates are superimposed.

2. Is the radial velocity of Barnard's Star positive or negative? What is the physical interpretation of a positive or negative radial velocity? Explain.

3. Which of the quantities V_r, T, and V could not be determined if a parallax could not be measured for a given star? Explain.

Data Sheet

d_μ

d_p

d_o

x_o

x_{line}

$\lambda_1 = 4404.75$ Å

$\lambda_2 = 4427.31$ Å

λ_{obs}

$\lambda_{lab} = 4415.13$ Å

V_r

μ

p

r

T

V

Experiment 11

Some Physical Properties of Stars

I. Introduction

One of the most important tools available to the stellar astronomer is the spectroscope, in which the light from a star is broken up into its component colors. The appearance of the resulting spectrum can then be used to infer a number of the physical properties of these distant suns. In this exercise you will obtain the temperature, luminosity, and radius of one such object.

II. Basic Data

The basic data for this exercise are presented in Table 11.1, in which parallax and apparent magnitude (m_*) data are listed for the eighteen stars whose spectra are shown in Figure 11.2.

III. Reductions

Remove Figure 11.2 from your text and compare the unknown stellar spectrum assigned to you by your instructor with the sequence of spectra shown in Figure 11.1. From the appearance of the unknown spectrum, estimate the surface temperature of your unknown star. Enter your result in your data sheet.

Compute the absolute magnitude M_* of your star using the following form of the distance modulus formula

$$(11.1) \quad M_* = m_* + 5 \log_{10} p + 5$$

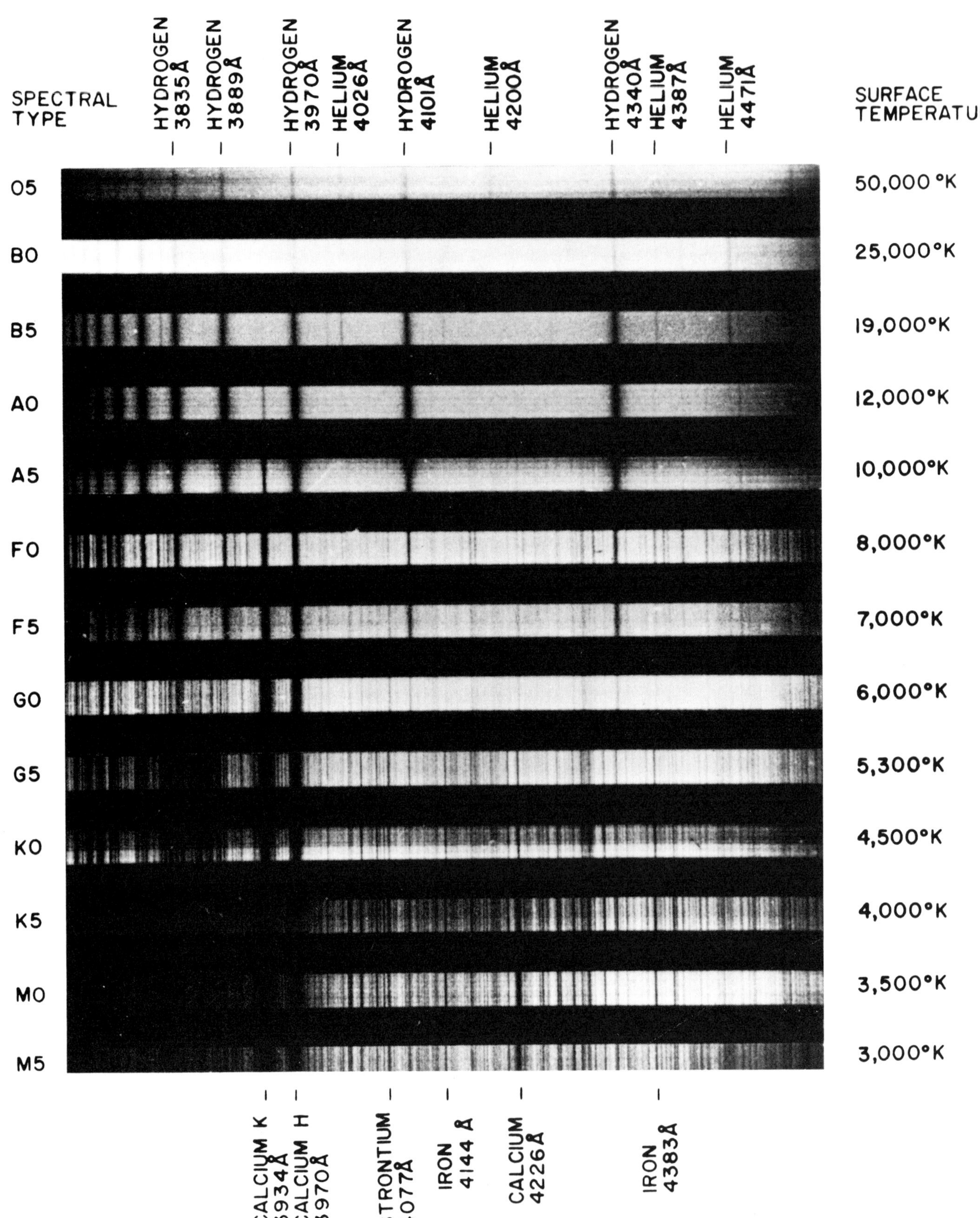
SPECTRAL TYPE
HYDROGEN 3835Å
HYDROGEN 3889Å
HYDROGEN 3970Å
HELIUM 4026Å
HYDROGEN 4101Å
HELIUM 4200Å
HYDROGEN 4340Å
HELIUM 4387Å
HELIUM 4471Å
SURFACE TEMPERATURE
O5
B0
B5
A0
A5
F0
F5
G0
G5
K0
K5
M0
M5
50,000 °K
25,000°K
19,000°K
12,000°K
10,000°K
8,000°K
7,000°K
6,000°K
5,300°K
4,500°K
4,000°K
3,500°K
3,000°K
CALCIUM K 3934Å
CALCIUM H 3970Å
STRONTIUM 4077Å
IRON 4144 Å
CALCIUM 4226Å
IRON 4383Å

FIGURE 11.1

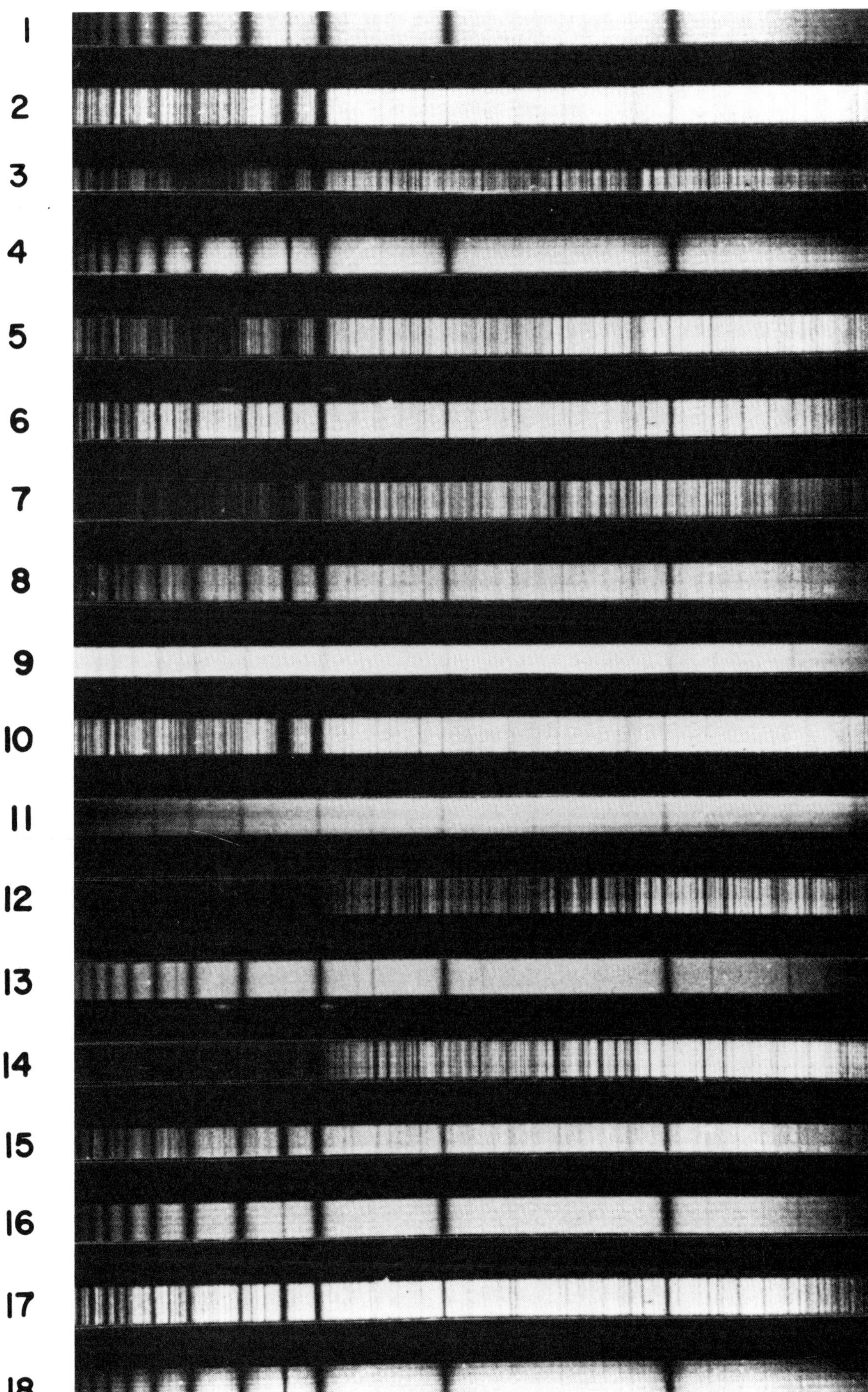

FIGURE 11.2

Table 11.1

Star	m_*	Parallax (arcseconds)	Star	m_*	Parallax (arcseconds)
1	2.4	.020	10	3.5	.182
2	4.3	.120	11	2.3	.001
3	3.5	.018	12	0.9	.048
4	4.0	.037	13	3.9	.027
5	3.4	.108	14	2.0	.043
6	4.7	.022	15	0.3	.288
7	3.1	.004	16	0.0	.123
8	1.8	.029	17	3.4	.009
9	2.8	.014	18	2.7	.029

and then the stellar luminosity L_* from the equation

$$(11.2) \quad \mathrm{Log}_{10} \{L_*/L_\odot\} = \frac{-1}{2.5} \{M_* - M_\odot\}$$

where $M_\odot$ is +4.84 and $L_\odot$ is equal to 4×10^{33} ergs/sec. Enter your results in your data sheet.

The stellar radius R_* can be expressed by the following relation

$$(11.3) \quad R_* = R_\odot \sqrt{\frac{L_* \, T_\odot^4}{L_\odot \, T_*^4}}$$

where $R_\odot$ is the radius of the sun and is equal to 7×10^{10} cm and $T_\odot$ is the sun's effective temperature and is equal to 5800°K. Calculate the radius of your unknown star, using Equation (11.3) and enter your result in your data sheet.

IV. Questions

1. Why do the spectra shown in Figure 11.1 change so much in spite of the fact that all of the stars shown have virtually identical compositions?

2. What has been assumed concerning the nature of stars in working through this exercise?

3. Describe the effect on the earth and its climate if your unknown star replaced the sun at the center of the solar system.

Data Sheet

Unknown Star Number

Spectral Type

Temperature (T_*)

Absolute Magnitude (M_*)

Luminosity (L_*)

Radius (R_*)

Experiment 12

The Method of Spectroscopic Parallax

I. Introduction

The accurate determination of stellar distances by the direct method of trigonometric parallax is limited to a comparatively few stars in the night sky. Astronomers therefore must resort to more indirect means of obtaining parallaxes and distances to stars. In this exercise, you will employ one such method, the method of spectroscopic parallax, to obtain the distance and parallax of a star.

II. Measurements

Using the spectra displayed in Figure 12.1, measure the width of each of the Ca II emission lines indicated by the pair of arrows. The measured parameter W is illustrated in Figure 12.2. The widths should be measured accurately for all five of the standard stars shown in Figure 12.1 as well as for one of the unknown stars assigned to you by your instructor. Record all of your measurements in your data sheet.

III. Reductions

Calculate the absolute magnitudes of the five standard stars listed in Table 12.1, using the following version distance modulus relation

$$M = m + 5 + 5 \log p \qquad (12.1)$$

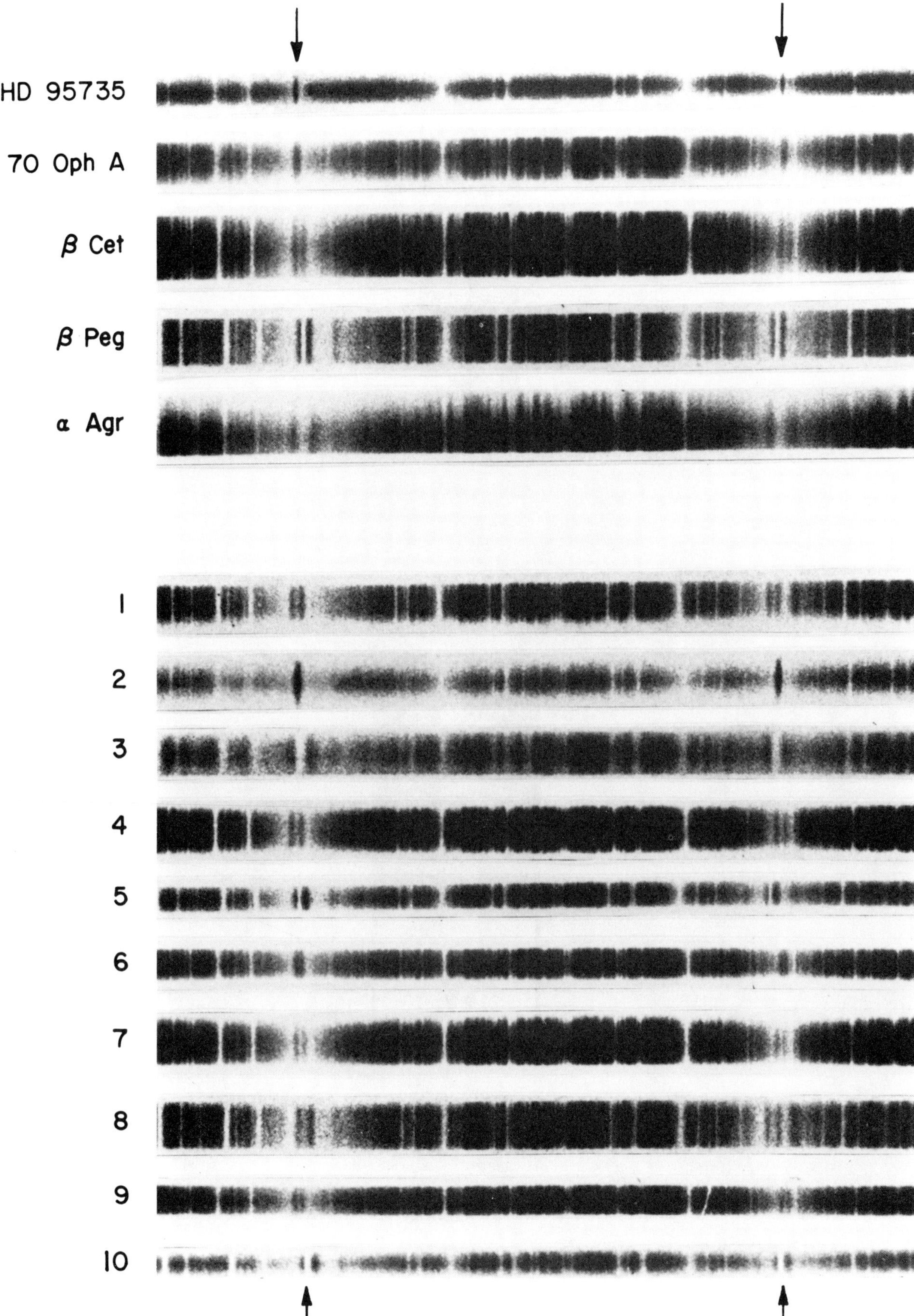

FIGURE 12.1

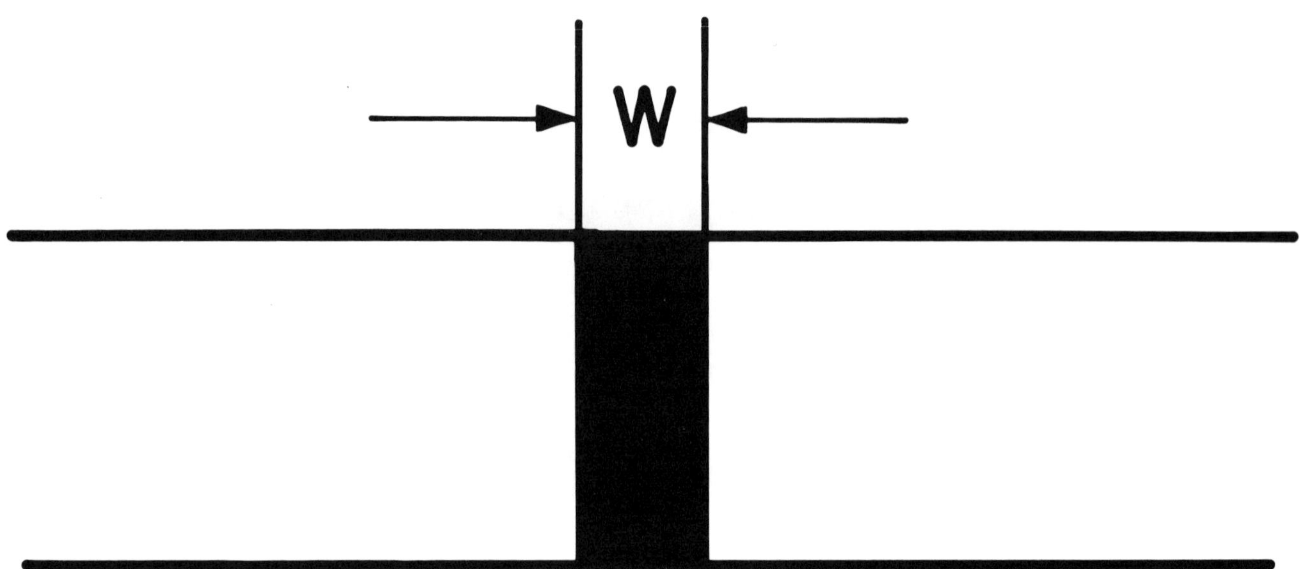

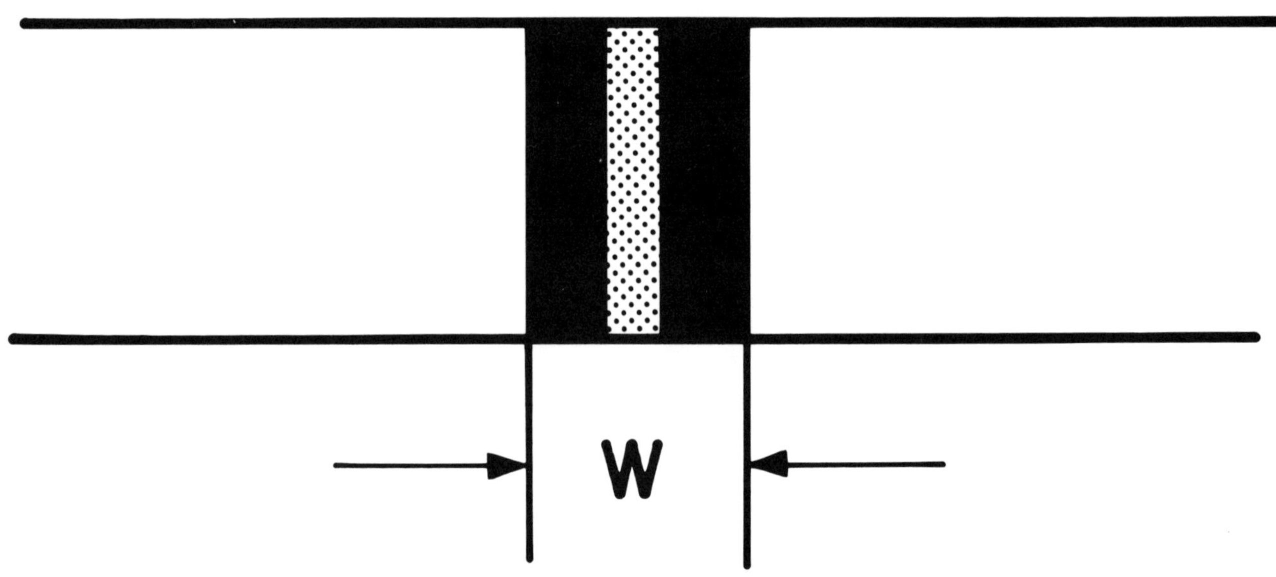

FIGURE 12.2

where m is the apparent magnitude and p is the trigonometric parallax. Plot the logarithm of the average $\bar{W}$ of the two W values versus the corresponding absolute magnitude for each of the five standard stars. Draw a straight line through the resulting points. Calculate the value of $\bar{W}$ for the calcium emission measured in your unknown star. From your log $\bar{W}$ versus M plot, find the value of M that corresponds to the log $\bar{W}$ value obtained for your unknown star. The value for the apparent magnitude m of your unknown star is listed in Table 12.2. Find the distance r to your unknown star by recalling that the distance in parsecs is equal to 1/parallax if the parallax is expressed in arcseconds.

Table 12.1

Data for the Standard Stars

Star	m	p(arcseconds)
HD 95735	7.5	0.398
70 Oph	4.1	0.188
β Cet	2.0	0.057
β Peg	2.6	0.015
α Aqr	3.2	0.003

Table 12.2

Star	m	Star	m
1	2.1	6	5.3
2	6.0	7	3.8
3	1.1	8	2.6
4	3.6	9	5.6
5	3.0	10	4.4

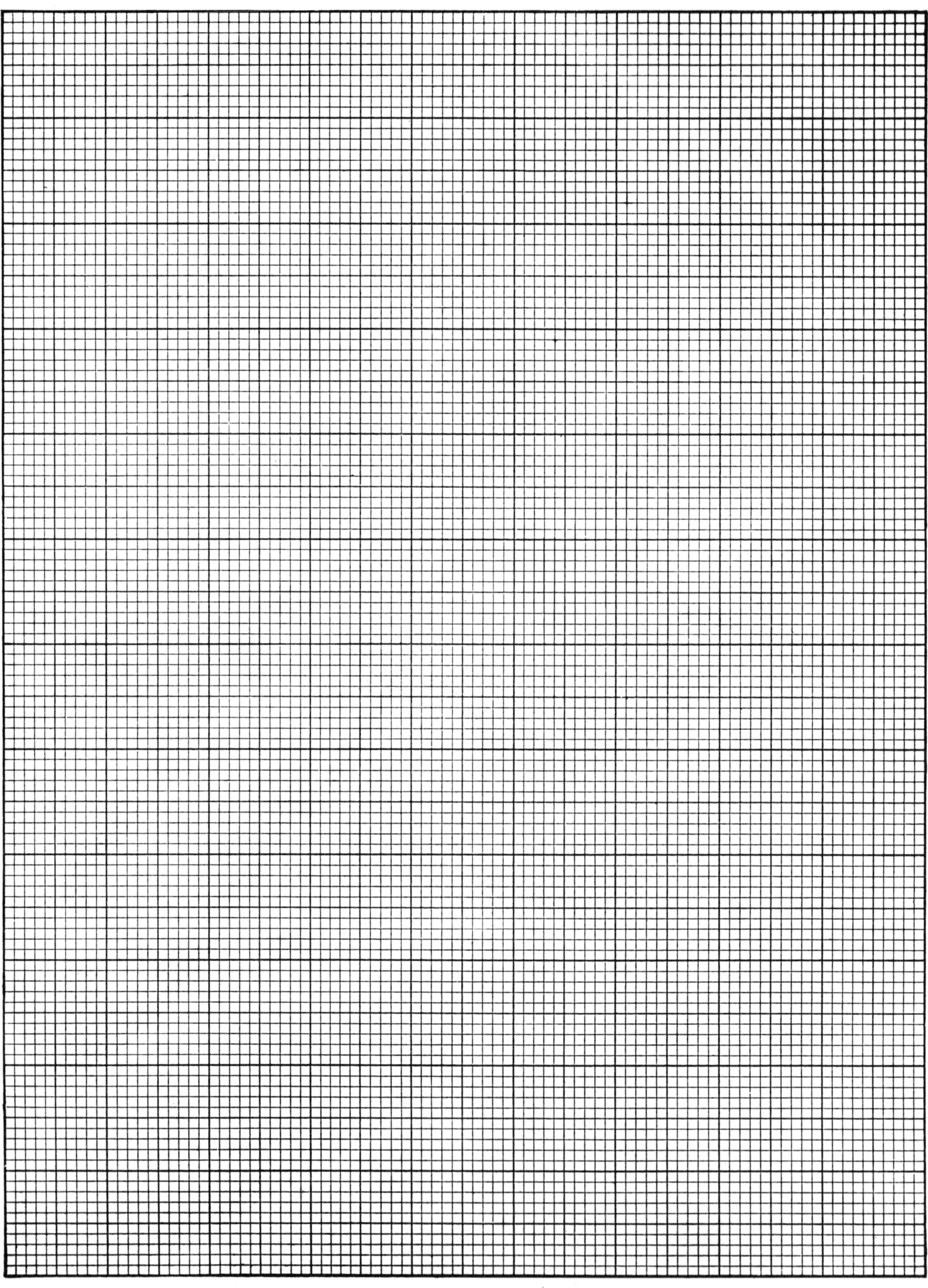

IV. Questions

1. What assumptions have been made in the determination of the spectroscopic parallax of your unknown star?

2. What are the advantages and disadvantages of this method of determining distances?

3. Estimate the uncertainty in your value of M for your unknown star.

Data Sheet

Star	W_1	W_2	$\bar{W}$	$\text{Log}(\bar{W})$	M
HD 95735					
70 Oph					
β Cet					
β Peg					
α Aqr					
Unknown Star					
p					
r					

Experiment 13

The Color-Magnitude Diagram for the Hyades

I. Introduction

One of the most important pieces of observational data that can be obtained for a star cluster is a plot of the colors of the stars in the cluster versus the apparent magnitude of the stars in the cluster. From such a diagram, called a color-magnitude diagram, it is possible to determine the distance and approximate age of a star cluster. In this exercise, you will investigate the color-magnitude for the Hyades, galactic cluster located in the constellation of Taurus.

II. Basic Data

The basic data for this exercise are listed in Tables 13.1 and 13.2. The first set of data consists of the absolute magnitudes and B-V colors for the "zero-age" main sequence, and the second set of data lists the apparent magnitudes and B-V colors for a number of stars in the Hyades cluster.

III. Reductions

Plot the V magnitudes versus the corresponding color index B-V for each of the Hyades stars listed in Table 13.1. The V magnitude should be plotted as the ordinate for this diagram. Note that the brighter stars have smaller numerical values of V, thus requiring decreasing V values on the positive y-axis. On a separate sheet graph paper and using the same scale as above, plot the zero-age main sequence data given in Table 13.2. Sketch a smooth curve through this set of points.

The color-magnitude diagram obtained for the Hyades should exhibit some sort of a main sequence. Keeping the B-V coordinates matched, fit as best you can the zero-age main sequence to the color-magnitude diagram for the Hyades. Read off the vertical shift Δ required for the fit. This observed shift is equal to the cluster's distance modulus. The distance r to the cluster is then

$$(13.1) \quad \text{Log}_{10}\ r = \frac{\Delta + 5}{5}$$

Calculate the distance r to the Hyades, and estimate your uncertainty from the uncertainty present in your main sequence fit. Enter your results in your data sheet.

To obtain the approximate age of the Hyades plot the Table 13.3 values of $\log_{10}$(age) versus the corresponding B-V color at which the main sequence turn-off point occurs for a given cluster age. Pass a smooth curve through your set of resulting points. From your color-magnitude diagram, determine the B-V color at which the Hyades main sequence departs from the zero-age main sequence. From your $\log_{10}$(age) versus B-V plot, read off the value of $\log_{10}$(age) that corresponds to the value of the B-V turn-off point that you obtained for the Hyades. Find the approximate age of the Hyades and enter your results in your data sheet.

Table 13.1

Photoelectric Data for Selected Members of the Hyades Cluster

Star	V	B-V
HD 24357	5.97	+0.34
HD 26462	5.73	+0.36
HD 26911	6.32	+0.40
HD 27176	5.65	+0.28
HD 27371	3.66	+0.99
HD 27397	5.59	+0.28
HD 27459	5.26	+0.22
HD 27697	3.76	+0.98
HD 27819	4.80	+0.16
HD 27934	4.22	+0.14
HD 27946	5.28	+0.25
HD 28305	3.54	+1.02
HD 28307	3.85	+0.96
HD 28319	3.41	+0.18
HD 28485	5.58	+0.32
HD 30780	5.10	+0.21
HD 32301	4.64	+1.45

Table 13.2

The Zero-Age Main Sequence

Mv	B-V	Mv	B-V
-2.10	-0.25	+1.74	+0.05
-1.10	-0.20	+2.00	+0.10
-0.30	-0.15	+2.45	+0.20
+0.50	-0.10	+2.95	+0.30
+1.10	-0.05	+3.56	+0.40
+1.50	+0.00	+4.23	+0.50

Table 13.3

B-V Turn-off Points for Various Star Cluster Ages

B-V Color of Turn-off Point	Log_{10}(age)
-0.4	6.5
-0.3	7.2
0.0	8.7
0.4	9.6
0.6	9.9
0.9	10.4
1.2	11.3

IV. Questions

1. Why do the bulk of the stars in the Hyades lie along the main sequence?

2. Explain why the turn-off point can be used in the determination of the age of the cluster.

3. Discuss the possible effect that the presence of gas and dust in the interstellar medium between the Sun and the Hyades would have on your results.

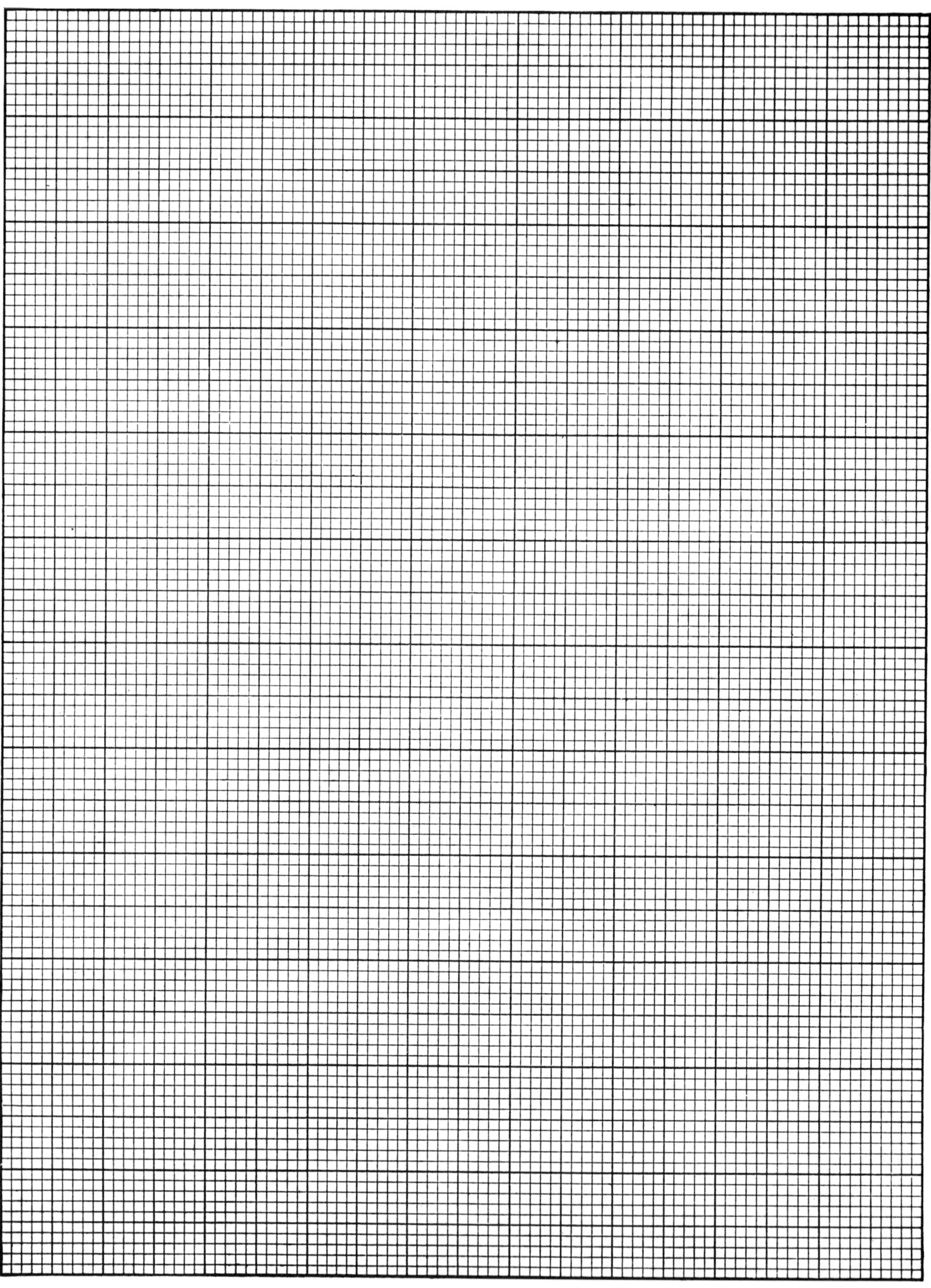

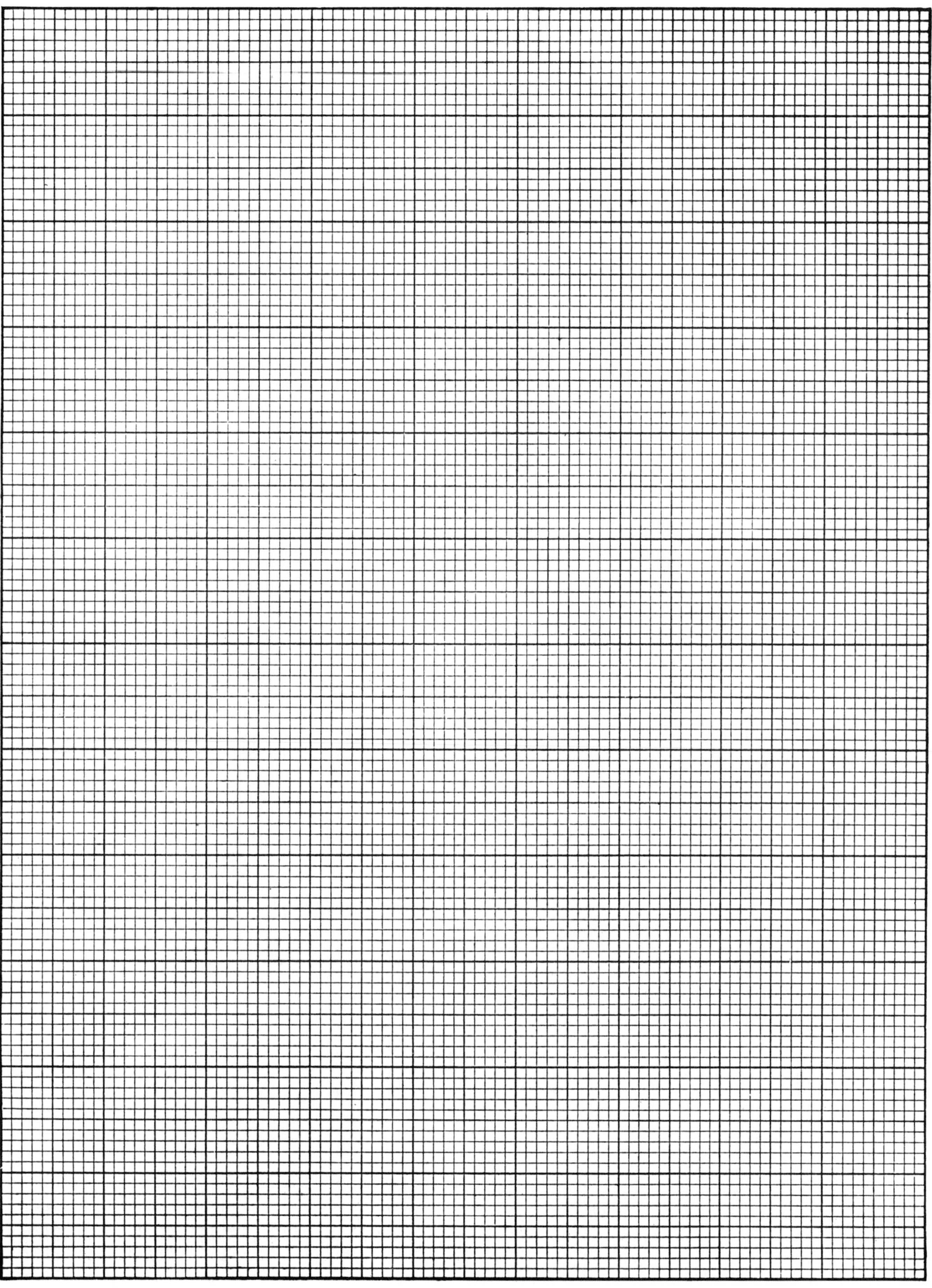

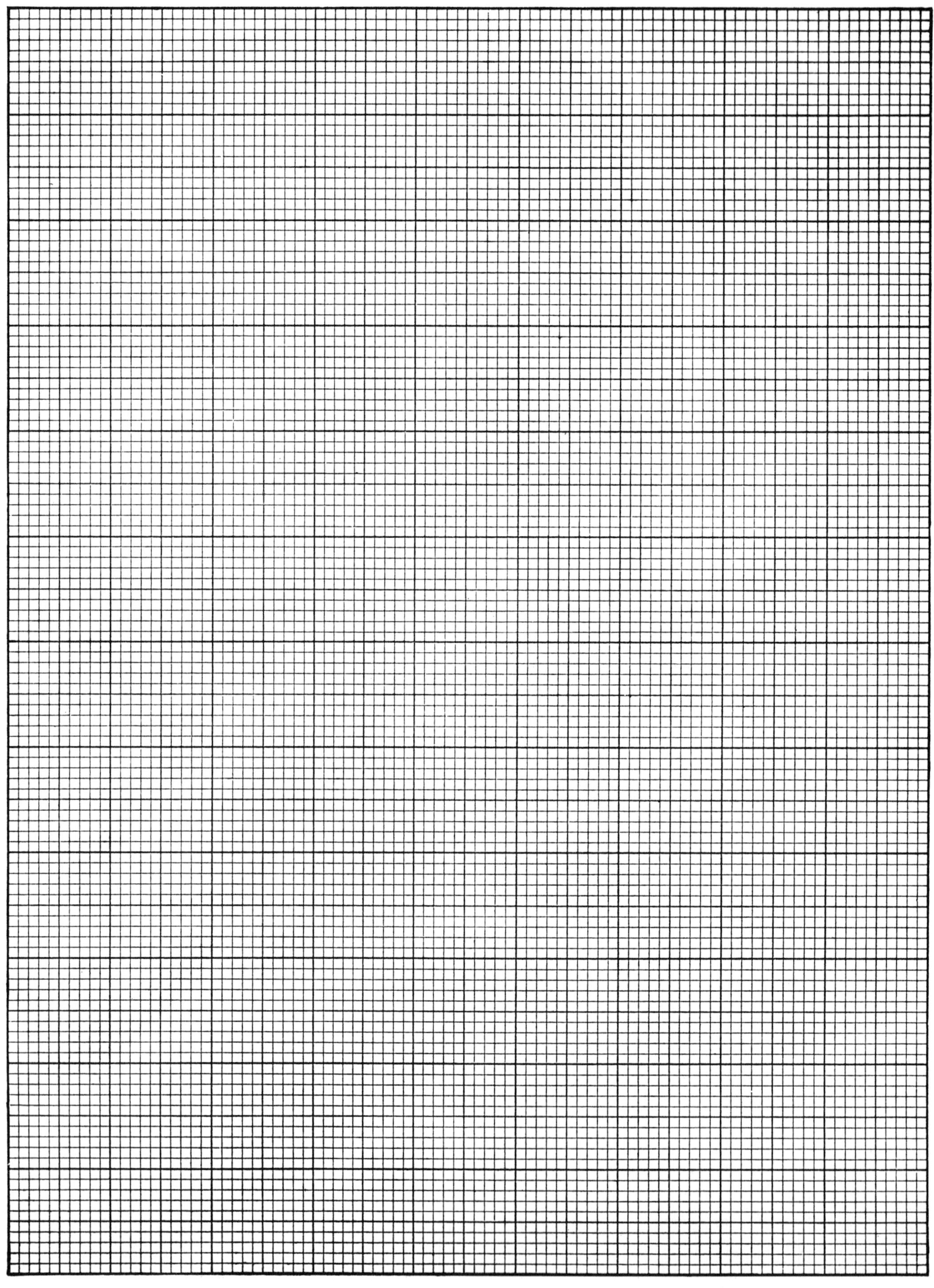

Data Sheet

Δ

Log r

r

log(Age)

Age

Experiment 14

The Distance and Absolute Magnitude of a Galactic Nova

I. Introduction

It is well known that nova outbursts are accompanied by rapidly expanding shells of gas which can often be detected by photographic means. In the following exercise you will employ the concepts of radial velocity, tangential motion, absolute magnitude, and distance modulus to investigate some of the properties of the exploding star Nova Aquilae.

II. Measurements

On the set of photographs shown in Figure 14.1, measure the diameter d of the outer shell of nebulosity on each picture as accurately as you can. In each case the image should be measured along several diameters and an average value taken for d. Measure also the length d_o of the 30 arcsecond scaling line shown in Figure 14.1.

Locate the H_δ emission feature on the nova's spectrum shown in Figure 14.2. Measure the distance x_o between the two comparison lines and the distance x_{line} between the shortward comparison line, in this case 3998.64, and the center of the absorption line immediately shortward of the nova's main H_δ emission feature (see Appendix 7).

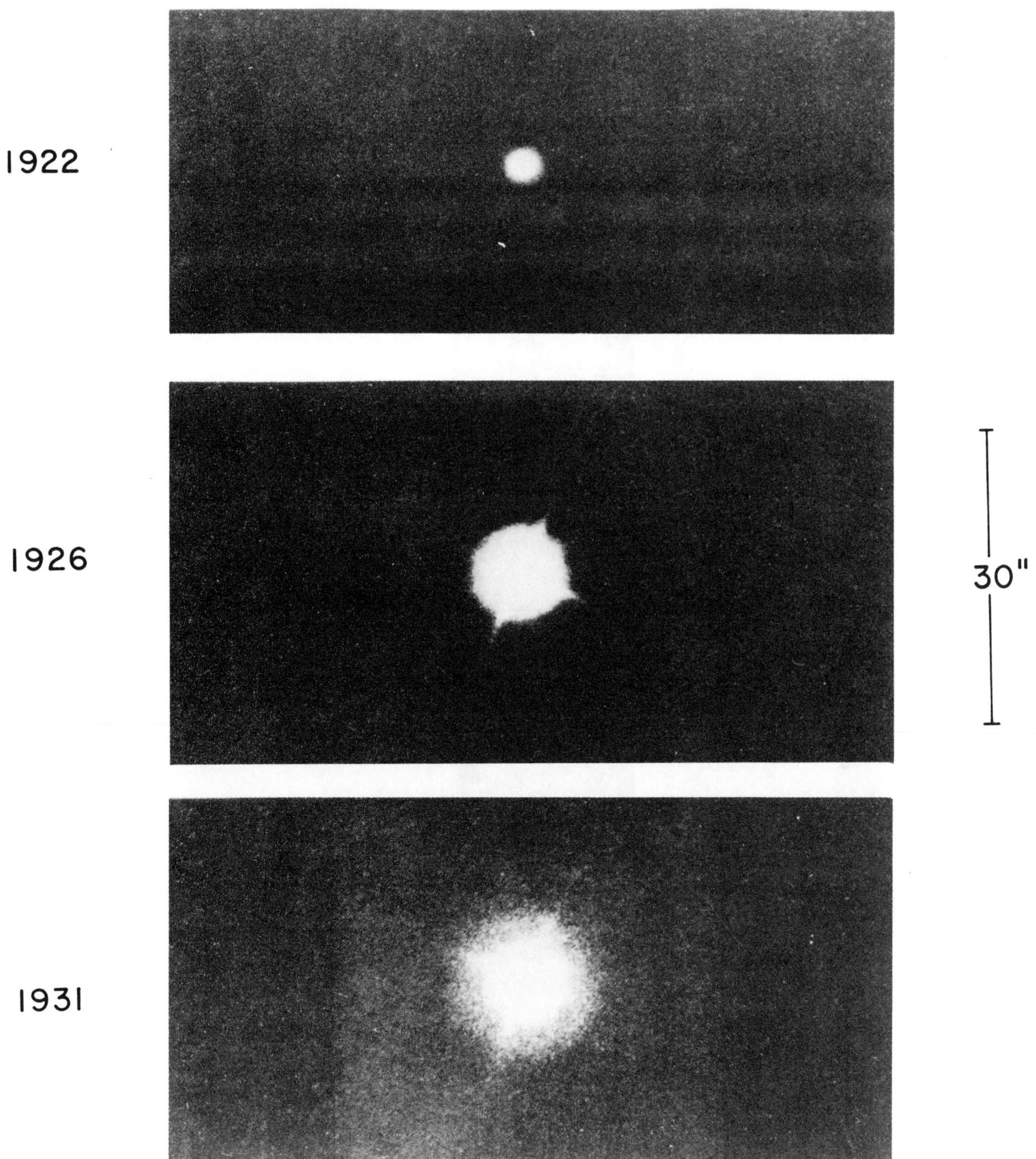

FIGURE 14.1

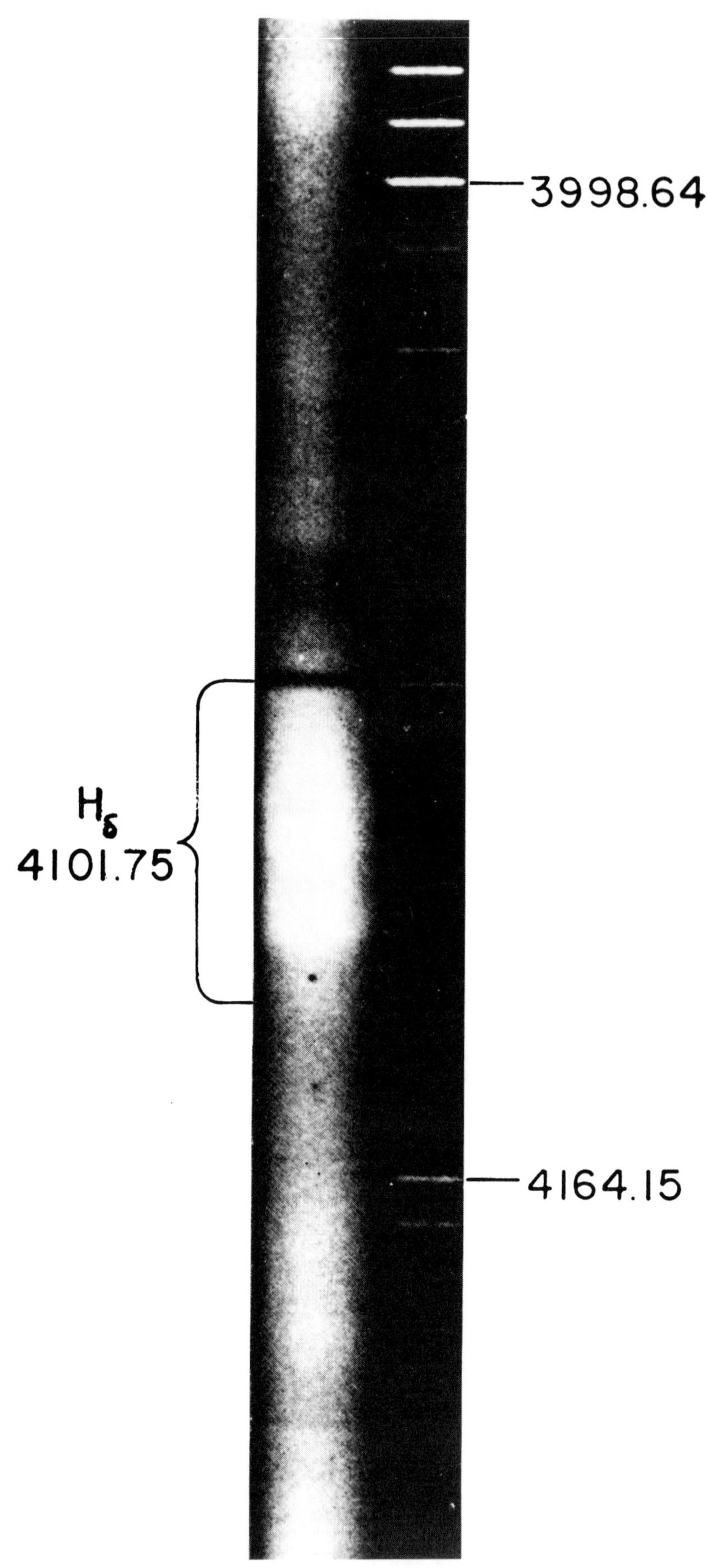

FIGURE 14.2

III. Reductions

Calculate the angular diameter α in arcseconds of each of the images in Figure 14.1, using the relationship that

$$(14.1) \quad \alpha = 30'' \frac{d}{d_o}$$

If λ_1 is the wavelength of the shortward iron comparison line, then the wavelength λ_{line} of the violet-side absorption line is

$$(14.2) \quad \lambda_{line} = \lambda_1 + \frac{\lambda_2 - \lambda_1}{x_o} x_{line}$$

where λ_2 is the longward of the two iron comparison lines used to measure x_o and in this case is equal to 4164.15 Å. The corresponding radial velocity V_r for the H_δ absorption feature is then

$$(14.3) \quad V_r = \frac{\lambda_{line} - \lambda_{lab}}{\lambda_{lab}} c$$

where λ_{lab} is the laboratory wavelength of the H_δ emission feature and is equal to 4101.75 Å. Calculate V_r for the given spectrogram and enter your results in your data sheet.

Plot the measured angular diameter for the expanding nebulosity about Nova Aquilae versus time. Draw a straight line through the resulting points and determine the slope s of the line in arcseconds/year. This value represents the mean rate of angular expansion of the nebulosity. The distance r to Nova Aquilae is then given by

$$(14.4) \quad r = \frac{1}{s} \frac{|V_r|}{4.75}$$

where r is in parsecs. Calculate r for Nova Aquilae and enter your result in your data sheet.

Calculate the absolute magnitude M of Nova Aquilae at maximum light using the distance modulus formula

$$(14.5) \quad M = m - 5 \log_{10} r + 5$$

and assuming that m was roughly equal to -1.2 at maximum light.

Determine from your α-t plot the time t_o at which Nova Aquilae had an angular diameter of zero. This value represents the time t_o of the initial outburst and should be recorded in your data sheet.

IV. Questions

1. What has been assumed about the nova while doing the analysis?

2. Explain why the violet absorption edge of the H_δ feature represents the velocity of the expanding gas shell.

3. A "guest star" or nova was reported in early June of 1918. Could this object be the remains of that event? Explain. How would you decide the issue for sure?

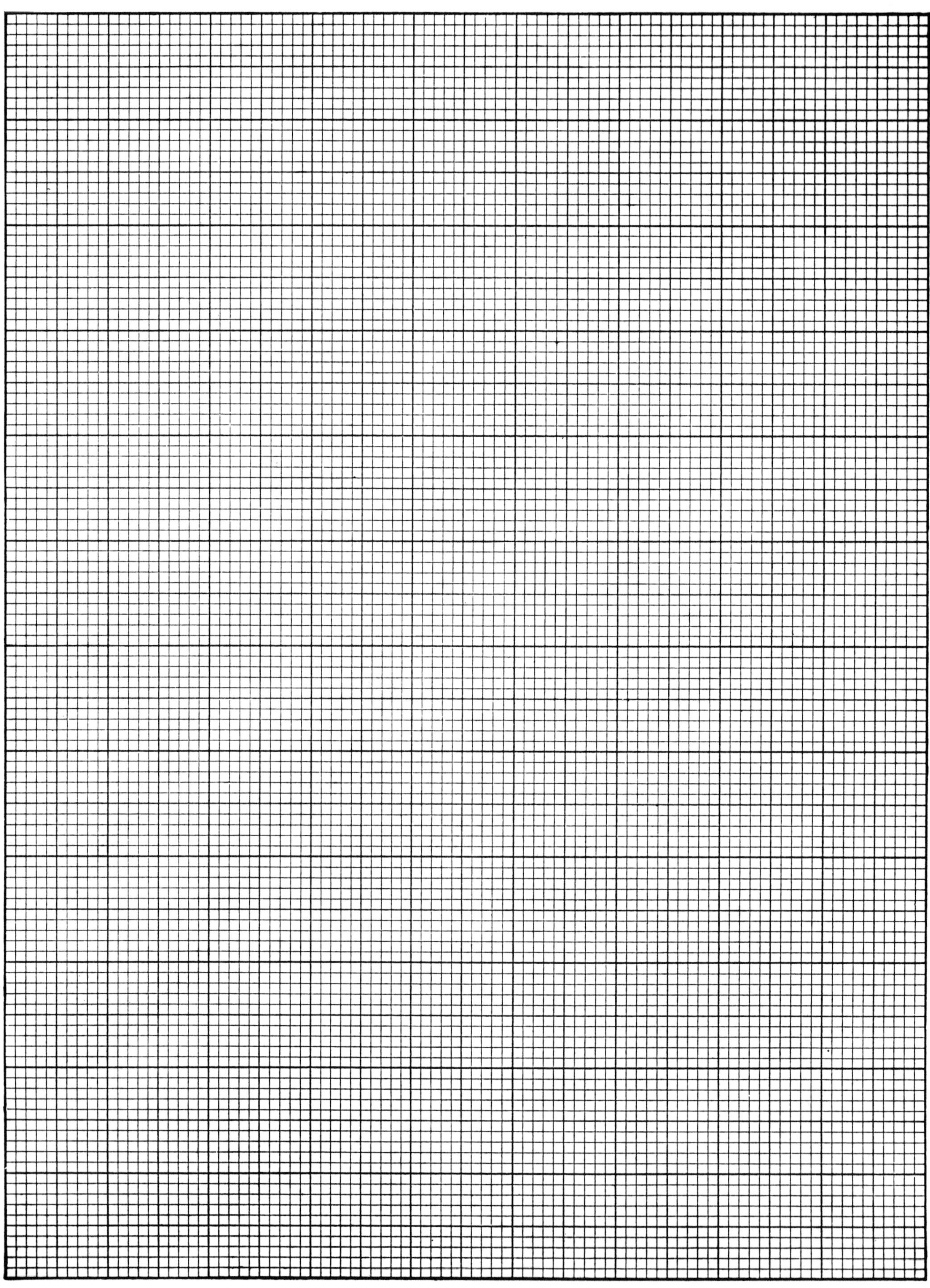

Data Sheet

d_o

d_1

d_2

d_3

α_1

α_2

α_3

μ

x_o

x_{line}

$\lambda_1 = 3998.64$ Å

$\lambda_2 = 4164.15$ Å

λ_{line}

$\lambda_{line} - \lambda_{lab}$

V_r

r

M

t_o

Experiment 15

The Wolf Diagram for the Horsehead Nebula

I. Introduction

Throughout the Milky Way plane lie clouds of obscuring matter which blot out the light from the stars behind them. Of the techniques developed to investigate these objects, one of the most ingenious is a method of star-count plotting that is referred to as the Wolf diagram. In this exercise you will find the distance to one such object, the Horsehead Nebula near the bright star Zeta Orionis, by constructing a Wolf diagram for this object.

II. Measurements

On the photograph of the Horsehead Nebula shown in Figure 15.1, measure the linear diameter d_6 of each of the four 6th magnitude stars and enter your results in your data sheet.

III. Reductions

Calculate the diameters d_i of the average size 7th, 8th, 9th, 10th and 11th magnitude stellar images in Figure 15.1 using the relations

$$
\begin{aligned}
(15.1)\quad d_7 &= 0.63\ d_6 \\
d_8 &= 0.63\ d_7 \\
d_9 &= 0.63\ d_8 \\
d_{10} &= 0.63\ d_9 \\
d_{11} &= 0.63\ d_{10}
\end{aligned}
$$

FIGURE 15.1

The expressions for the lower limit diameters for a 1.0 magnitude interval centered on a given magnitude are presented in Table 15.1 and should be used to calculate each of the limits. Enter your results in your data sheet.

Table 15.1

Mean Magnitude of Interval	Magnitude Range	Lower Limit Diameter
6.0	5.5-6.5	$\frac{d_6 + d_7}{2}$
7.0	6.5-7.5	$\frac{d_7 + d_8}{2}$
8.0	7.5-8.5	$\frac{d_8 + d_9}{2}$
9.0	8.5-9.5	$\frac{d_9 + d_{10}}{2}$
10.0	9.5-10.5	$\frac{d_{10} + d_{11}}{2}$

In the high star-count region (right side) of Figure 15.1 count up the <u>total</u> number of stars $N_T(m)$ that have diameters larger than the lower limit diameter for each of the magnitude intervals. Construct the Wolf diagram for the Horsehead Nebula by plotting $\log_{10} N_T(m)$ versus the mean magnitude m of the interval. On the same graph, repeat the plot for the low count $N_T'(m)$ data. Measure the magnitude m_o at which the N_T' curve diverges from the N_T plot. Assuming that the mean absolute magnitude of the stars in this region of the sky is equal to -1.0, the distance r to the Horsehead Nebula is then

$$(15.2) \quad \mathrm{Log}_{10}(r) = \frac{m_o + 6}{5}$$

Calculate the distance to the Horsehead Nebula and enter the result in your data sheet.

IV. Questions

1. Why are there fewer stars to the left of the boundary in Figure 15.1?

2. Explain why the star-count plots diverge at m_o.

3. If the star counts were continued to fainter magnitudes, describe the behavior of the two star-count plots.

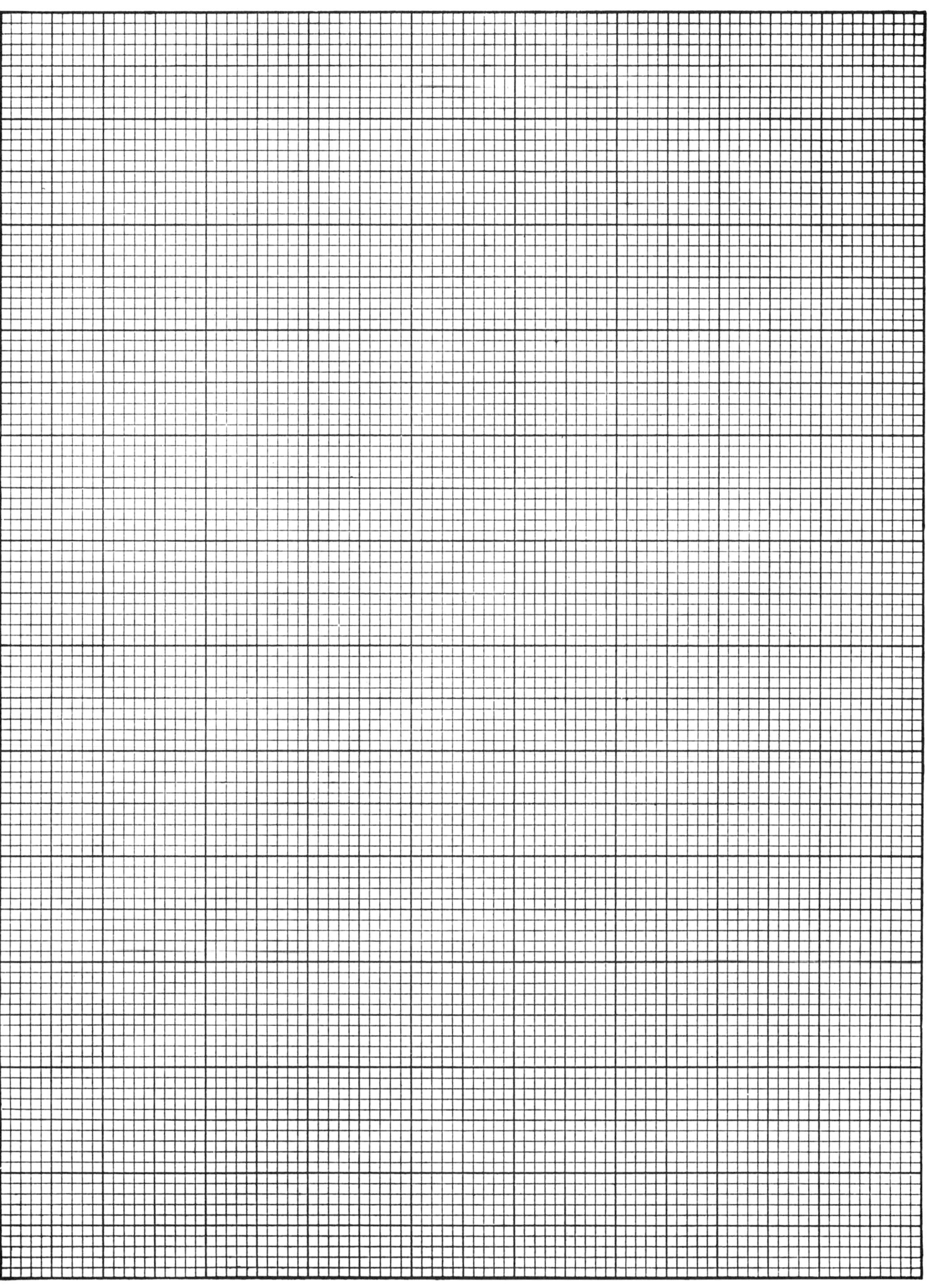

Data Sheet

d_6	d_7	d_8	d_9	d_{10}

Mean Magnitude	Magnitude Interval	Lower Limit Diameter
6.0	5.5-6.5	
7.0	6.5-7.5	
8.0	7.5-8.5	
9.0	8.5-9.5	
10.0	9.5-10.5	

Mean Magnitude	$N_T(m)$	$Log_{10}\{N_T(m)\}$	$N_T'(m)$	$Log_{10}\{N_T'(m)\}$
6.0				
7.0				
8.0				
9.0				
10.0				

m_o

$Log_{10} r$

r

Experiment 16

Properties of the Milky Way Galaxy

I. Introduction

Early in this century astronomers deduced that the sun is a part of a vast system of stars, the Milky Way Galaxy, which is thousands of light years across. In this exercise you will investigate some of the basic properties of our home galaxy, using observations of three globular clusters which lie along the galactic equator.

II. Measurements

Measure the linear diameter d_c of each of the globular clusters shown in Figure 16.1 as well as the length d_o of the 220' scaling line.

III. Reductions

For each of the globular clusters shown in Figure 16.1, calculate the distance r in parsecs to the cluster, using the relation

$$(16.1) \quad r = \frac{2.06 \times 10^5}{13,200} \frac{d_o}{d_c} D_o$$

where D_o is the average diameter of a globular cluster and is assumed to be 100 parsecs.

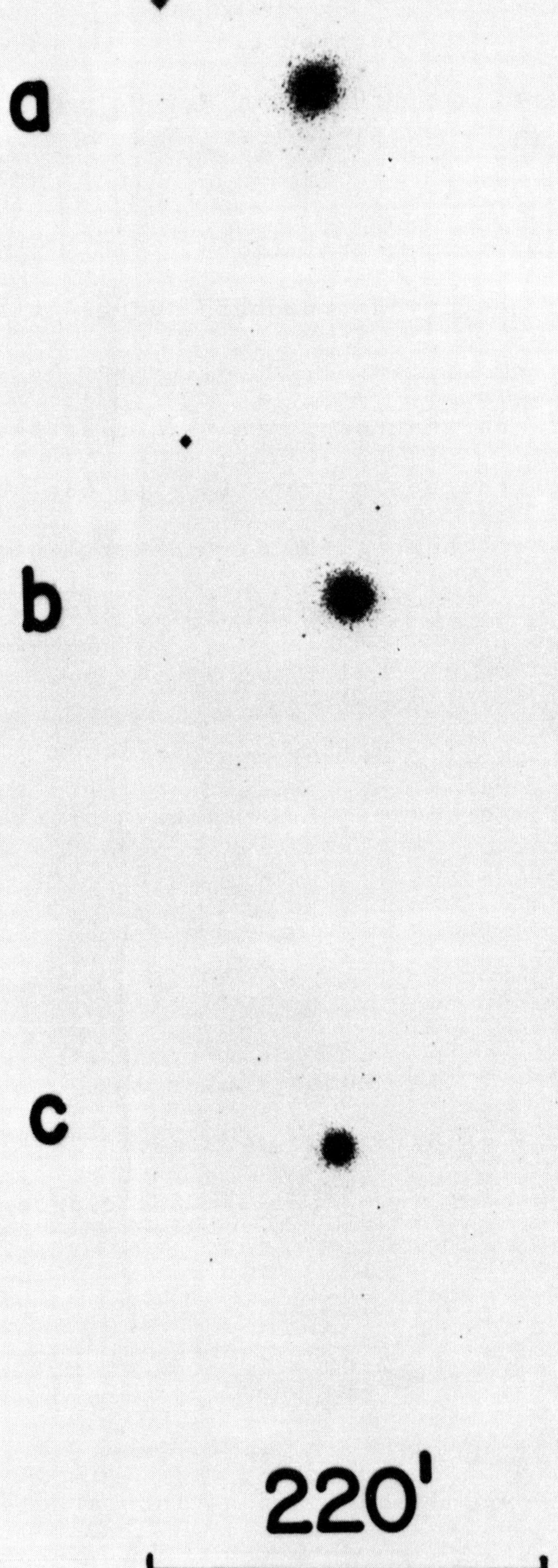

FIGURE 16.1

Using the data listed in Table 16.1, plot the calculated cluster distance versus the corresponding galactic longitude ℓ for each cluster in polar coordinates. Find the geometric center of the globular clusters and determine the length r_o between the sun (origin of the polar coordinate system) and the geometric center of the cluster array. The distance so determined is the radius of the solar orbit about the nucleus of the Galaxy. This result should be converted into both astronomical units and kilometers, and the values entered in your data sheet.

Table 16.1

Cluster	ℓ	V_c (km/sec)
a	283°	+191
b	62°	-145
c	0°	0

For each of the two clusters having non-zero radial velocities in Table 16.1, determine the solar velocity $V_\odot$ using the relation

$$(16.2) \quad V_\odot = \frac{|V_c|}{\cos\theta} + 80 \text{ km/sec}$$

where V_c is the observed radial velocity of the cluster given in Table 16.1, and $\theta = \ell - 270°$ for $V_c > 0$, and $\theta = \ell - 90°$ for $V_c < 0$. The 80 km/sec term is the approximate value of the mean rotation rate of the globular clusters relative to the center of the Galaxy. Calculate the average value for $V_\odot$ from your two non-zero radial velocity clusters and determine the period $P_\odot$ in seconds of the solar revolution about the center of the Galaxy from the relation

$$(16.3) \quad P_{\odot} = \frac{2\pi r_o}{V_{\odot}}$$

where r_o is in km and $V_{\odot}$ is in km/sec. Calculate the mass of the Galaxy M_G in solar masses, using Kepler's Harmonic Law

$$(16.4) \quad M_G = \frac{r_o^3}{P_{\odot}^2}$$

where r_o is in astronomical units and $P_{\odot}$ is now expressed in years. Enter all of your results in your data sheet.

IV. Questions

1. What have we assumed concerning the distribution of the globular clusters with respect to the Milky Way Galaxy?

2. Find the total diameter of the Milky Way Galaxy. Clearly indicate any assumptions that you make.

3. Estimate the total number of stars in the Milky Way Galaxy. Clearly indicate the assumptions that you make.

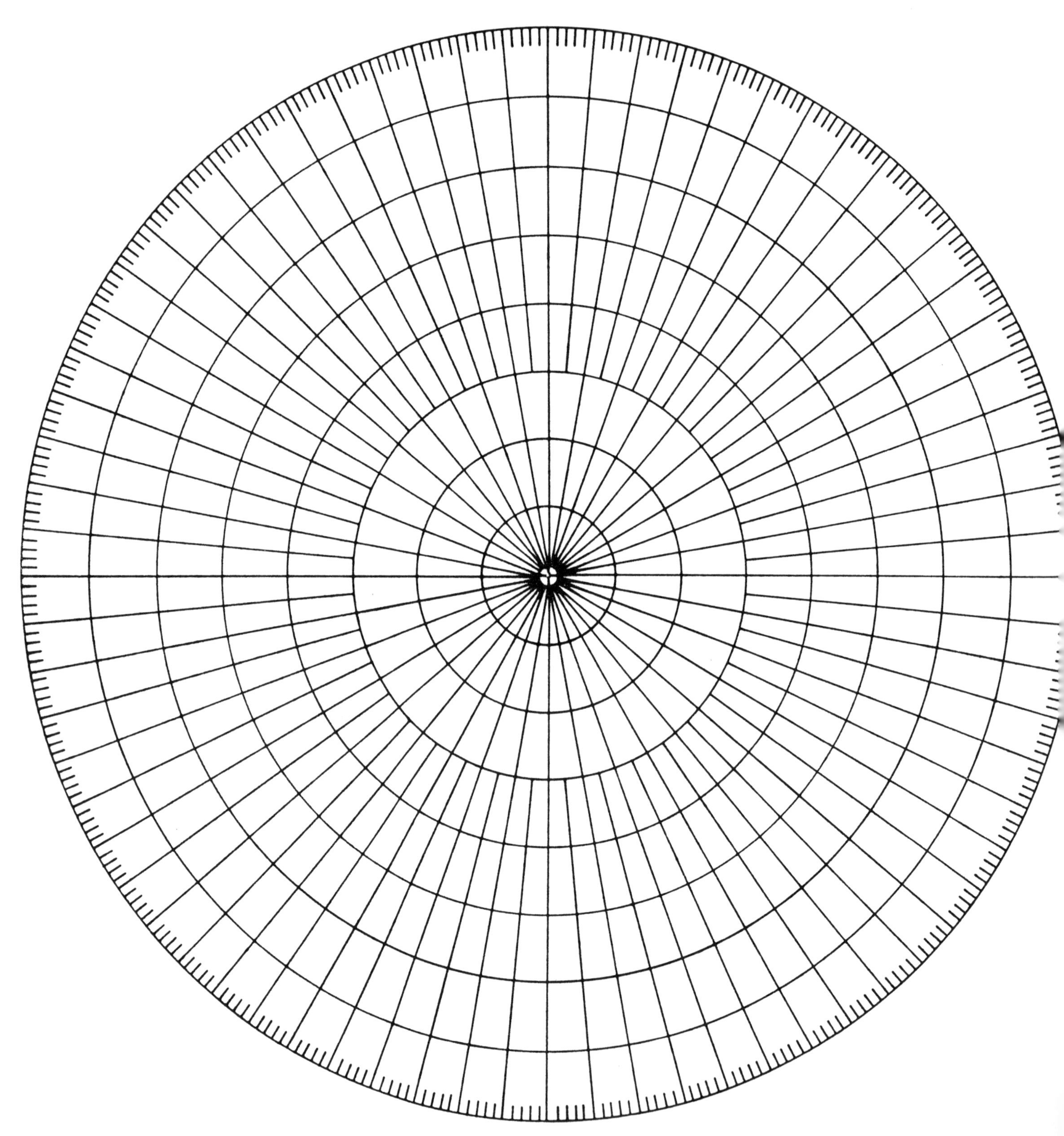

Data Sheet

d_o

D = 100 parsecs

Cluster	d_c (mm)	r (pc)
a		
b		
c		

r_o

r_o(AU)

r_o(km)

$|V_{1\Theta}|$

$|V_{2\Theta}|$

$\bar{V}_\Theta$

P_Θ(sec)

P_Θ(yr)

M_G

Experiment 17

The Distance to the Galaxy M 87

I. Introduction

The distances to the galaxies, even to the relatively nearby systems, are so vast that the methods of trigonometric parallax used for determining fundamental stellar distances are totally inadequate for obtaining intergalactic distances. As a result, astronomers must resort to more indirect methods of distance determination. Perhaps the most reliable of these methods is the use of the so-called distance indicators or objects whose intrinsic brightnesses are known and which have been identified in other galaxies. By comparing the known absolute magnitude of a given distance indicator with the measured apparent magnitude of the same type of object which has been located in another galaxy, astronomers can determine the distance to the galaxy, using the distance modulus relation. In this exercise you will determine the distance to the galaxy M 87, using one such distance indicator, the globular clusters.

II. Measurements

On the photograph shown in Figure 17.1, measure the diameter d_* of each of the comparison stars whose magnitudes are marked as well as the diameters dc of at least five of the globular clusters indicated by your instructor. The measurements should be performed as carefully and as accurately as possible owing to the small image sizes. Enter your results in your data sheet.

FIGURE 17.1

III. Reductions

Plot the value of $\log_{10} d_*^2$ versus the corresponding apparent magnitude for each of the comparison stars employed in this exercise and fit a straight line through the resulting points. Calculate the squares of the diameters of the globular clusters measured. For each cluster find the value of the apparent magnitude m corresponding to the measured value of $\log_{10} (d_c^2)$ for that cluster using the calibration curve just constructed. Find the mean value $\bar{m}$ of the globular clusters measured, and enter your result in your data sheet.

Assuming that the mean absolute magnitude of the brighter globular clusters located about M 87 is equal to -9.0, the distance r to M 87 is then given by the following variation of the distance modulus formula

$$(17.1) \quad \text{Log}_{10}\ r = \frac{\bar{m} + 14}{5}$$

Using Equation (17.1), calculate the distance to M 87, and enter your result in your data sheet.

Table 17.1

Apparent Magnitudes of the Comparison Stars in Figure 17.1

Star Number	m_V
1	20.3
2	21.8
3	22.7
4	23.5
5	24.2

IV. Questions

1. Discuss the basic assumptions made in this method of distance determination.

2. Suppose that some of the globular clusters measured were on the far side of M 87. Describe the effect that this would have on your results.

3. How does the distribution of the globular clusters relative to the center of M 87 compare with that of the Milky Way Galaxy?

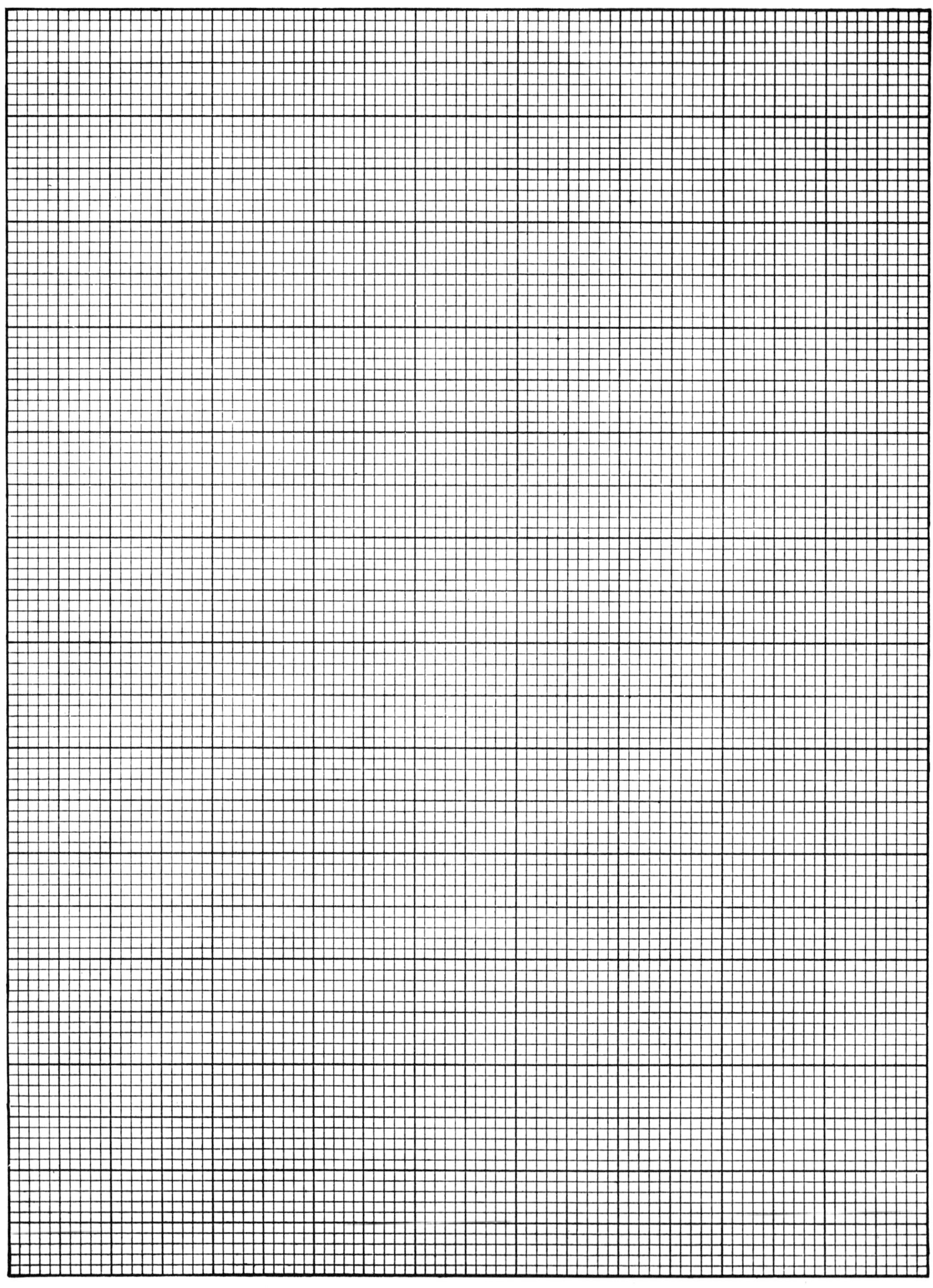

Data Sheet

Star	m	d_* (mm)	d_*^2	$\log_{10}(d_*^2)$
1				
2				
3				
4				
5				

Globular Cluster	d_c (mm)	d_c^2	$\log_{10}(d_c^2)$	m
1				
2				
3				
4				
5				

$\bar{m}$

$\log_{10} r$

r

Experiment 18

The Rotation and Mass of the Andromeda Galaxy M 31

I. Introduction

Astronomical spectroscopy is one of the most powerful and versatile tools available to the observational astronomer. In this exercise one use of spectroscopy will be demonstrated as you investigate the rotational properties of the nearby galaxy M 31 in the constellation of Andromeda.

II. Basic Data

The basic data for this experiment are listed in Table 18.1 in which the radial velocities of various regions of M 31 are listed along with the position of the region relative to that galaxy's nucleus.

III. Reductions

Plot the radial velocities listed in Table 18.1 versus their corresponding angular distances ρ from the nucleus and sketch a smooth curve through the resulting points. From your curve find the value of the radial velocity V_o at $\rho = 0$ or zero angular separation. The value of V_o so determined represents the velocity of the entire system and should be subtracted from each velocity listed in Table 18.1 to yield V_r', the velocity of a given region relative to the nucleus of M 31.

Plot V_r' versus the separation from the nucleus and sketch a smooth curve through the resulting points. Select a point toward the outer regions ($|\rho| > 80'$) of the rotation curve and read off its (V_r', ρ) coordinates. Compute the linear distance a in AU between the nucleus and the given point using

$$(18.1) \qquad a = \frac{60r\rho}{206265}$$

where r is the distance to M 31 and is equal to 9×10^{10} AU. Having obtained a for the given point, convert this value to km and find the period of revolution P in seconds from

$$(18.2) \qquad P = \frac{2\pi a}{V_r'}$$

Convert your value of P into years and calculate both a^3 and P^2 for the given point using the value of a as measured in AU's. Repeat the above process for five different points on the outer parts of the rotation curve. Plot a^3 versus P^2 for your calculated values using a^3 as the ordinate. Draw a straight line through the plotted points and determine the slope of the line. This value of the slope so determined is equal to the mass of M 31, $M_{M\ 31}$ in solar masses. Enter your result in your data sheet.

Table 18.1

Point	ρ	V_r	Point	ρ	V_r
1	-120'	-460 km/sec	24	+2'	-250 km/sec
2	-100	-500	25	+2	-250
3	-96	-530	26	+6	-220
4	-80	-600	27	+5	-210
5	-65	-580	28	+4	-205
6	-70	-570	29	+10	-260
7	-50	-530	30	+12	-250
8	-29	-480	31	+12	-210
9	-30	-440	32	+14	-180
10	-25	-415	33	+15	-180
11	-20	-390	34	+16	-170
12	-16	-360	35	+22	-125
13	-15	-340	36	+21	-100
14	-13	-340	37	+28	-120
15	-10	-310	38	+29	-120
16	-8	-350	39	+46	0
17	-7	-330	40	+66	+70
18	-6	-370	41	+70	+60
19	-3	-360	42	+80	+100
20	-3	-340	43	+96	+80
21	-2	-305	44	+100	+30
22	+8	-290	45	+107	-50
23	+5	-280	46	+120	-50

IV. Questions

1. Show why V_o as it is defined in the exercise is the velocity of the entire M 31 system.

2. Discuss the shape of the rotation curve.

3. Why do you suppose that the points used in the mass determination of M 31 are taken from the outer portions of the rotation curve?

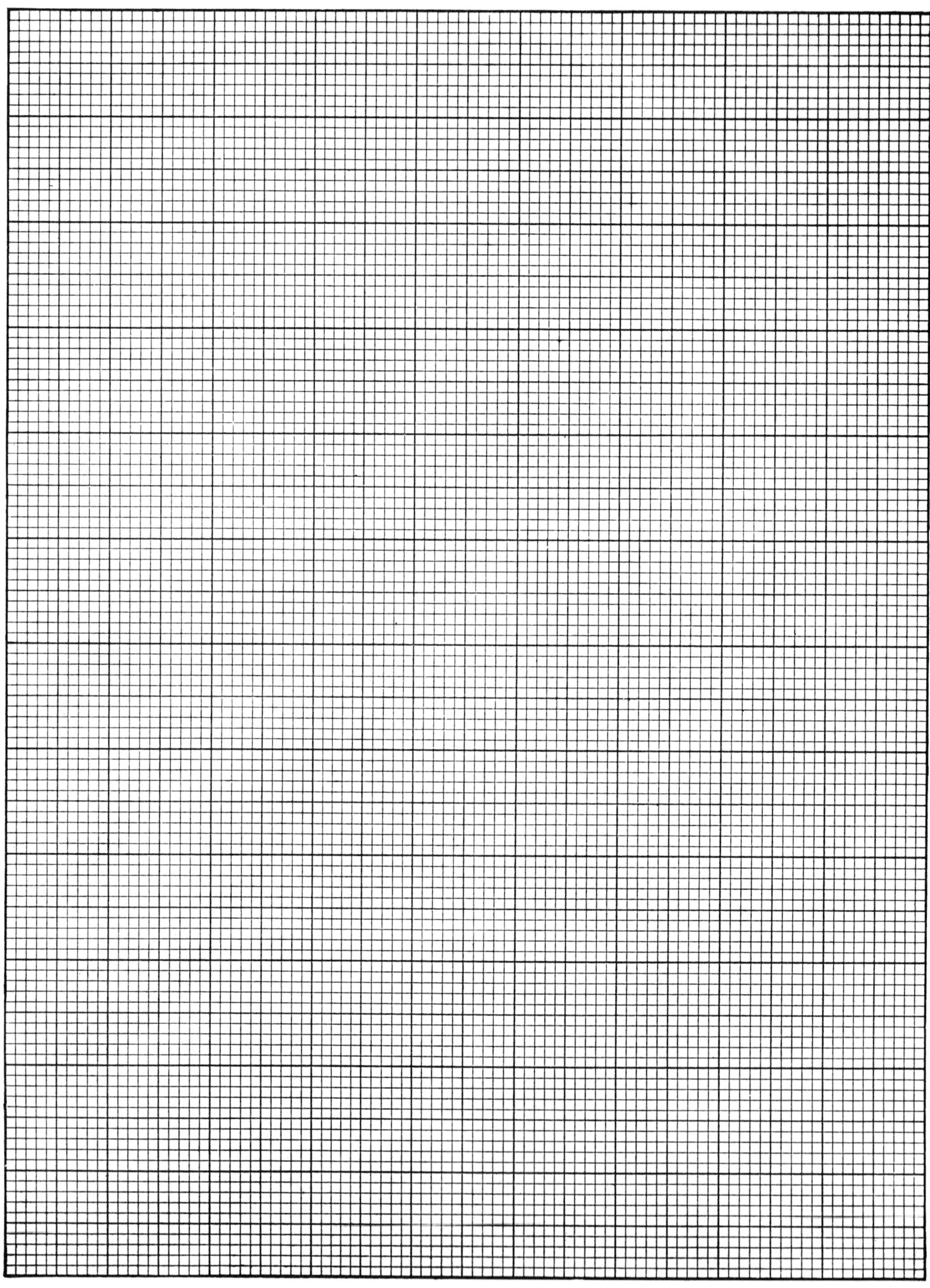

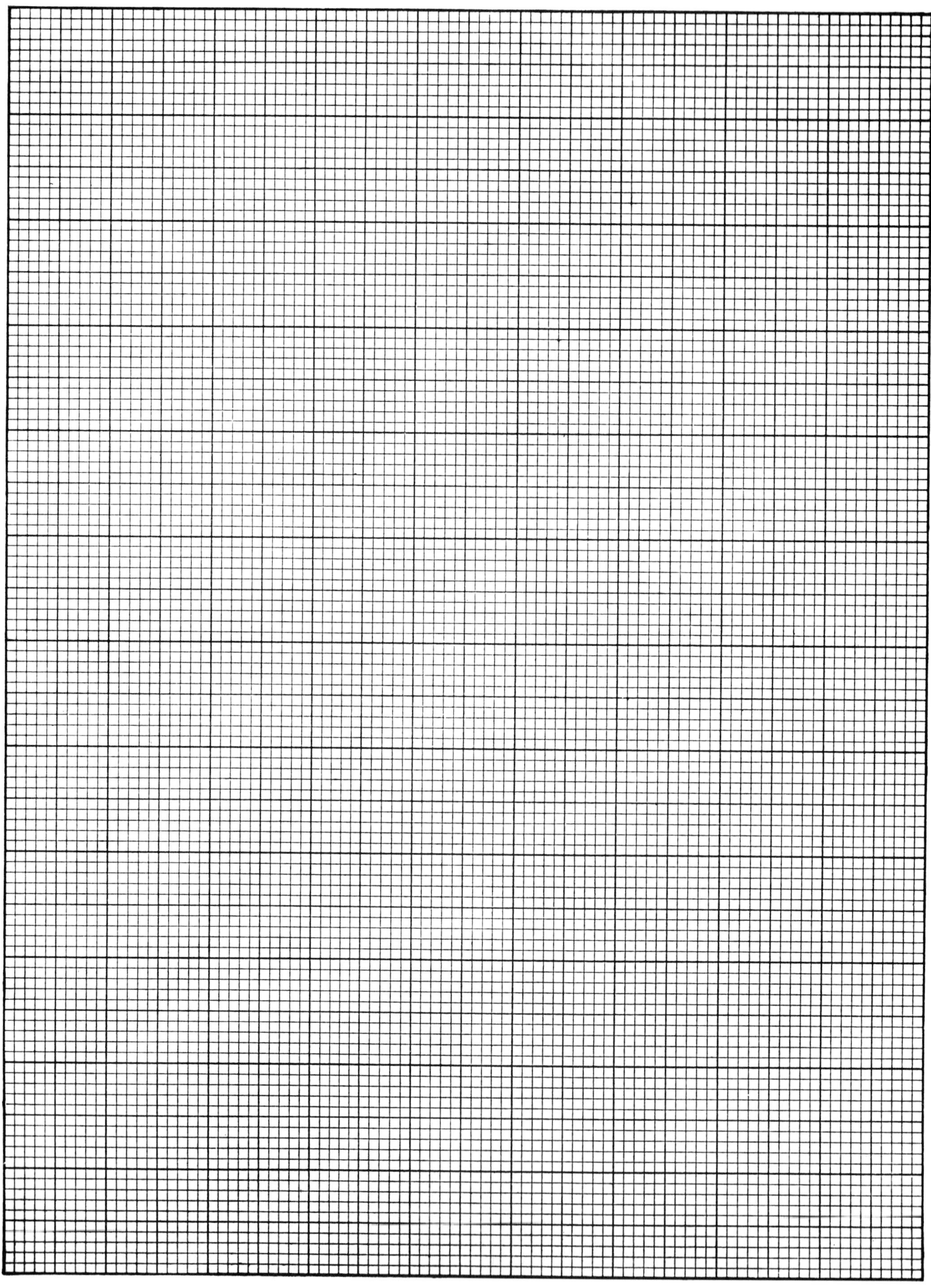

Data Sheet

V_o

Point	ρ	V_r'	Point	ρ	V_r'
1			24		
2			25		
3			26		
4			27		
5			28		
6			29		
7			30		
8			31		
9			32		
10			33		
11			34		
12			35		
13			36		
14			37		
15			38		
16			39		
17			40		
18			41		
19			42		
20			43		
21			44		
22			45		
23			46		

Position	1	2	3	4	5	6
ρ (' of arc)						
V_r' (km/sec)						
a (AU)						
a (km)						
P (sec)						
P (yr)						
a^3						
P^2						

Slope = $\mathcal{M}_{M\ 31}$ =

Experiment 19

A Determination of the Hubble Constant

I. Introduction

In the course of his investigation of the exterior galaxies, the American astronomer Edwin Hubble found that all of the galaxies outside of the local group were receding from the Milky Way Galaxy at velocities that become larger with increasing distance. This law, called the Hubble Law, is a most important relationship to the astronomer not only because it provides a useful method of determining extragalactic distances, but also because its behavior at great distances from the earth theoretically can provide important clues concerning the overall properties of the visible universe. In this exercise, you will examine some of the properties of this relationship.

II. Measurements

Measure the length d_o of the 720" scaling line shown in Figure 19.1 as well as the diameters d_G of each of the galaxies. Enter your results in your data sheet.

For each of the five galaxy spectra shown in Figure 19.1, measure the length x_o of the distance between the comparison lines a and b and the distances x_K and x_H between the two calcium absorption lines and the comparison line a, recalling that the K-line has the shorter wavelength (see Appendix 7). Enter all of your results in your data sheet.

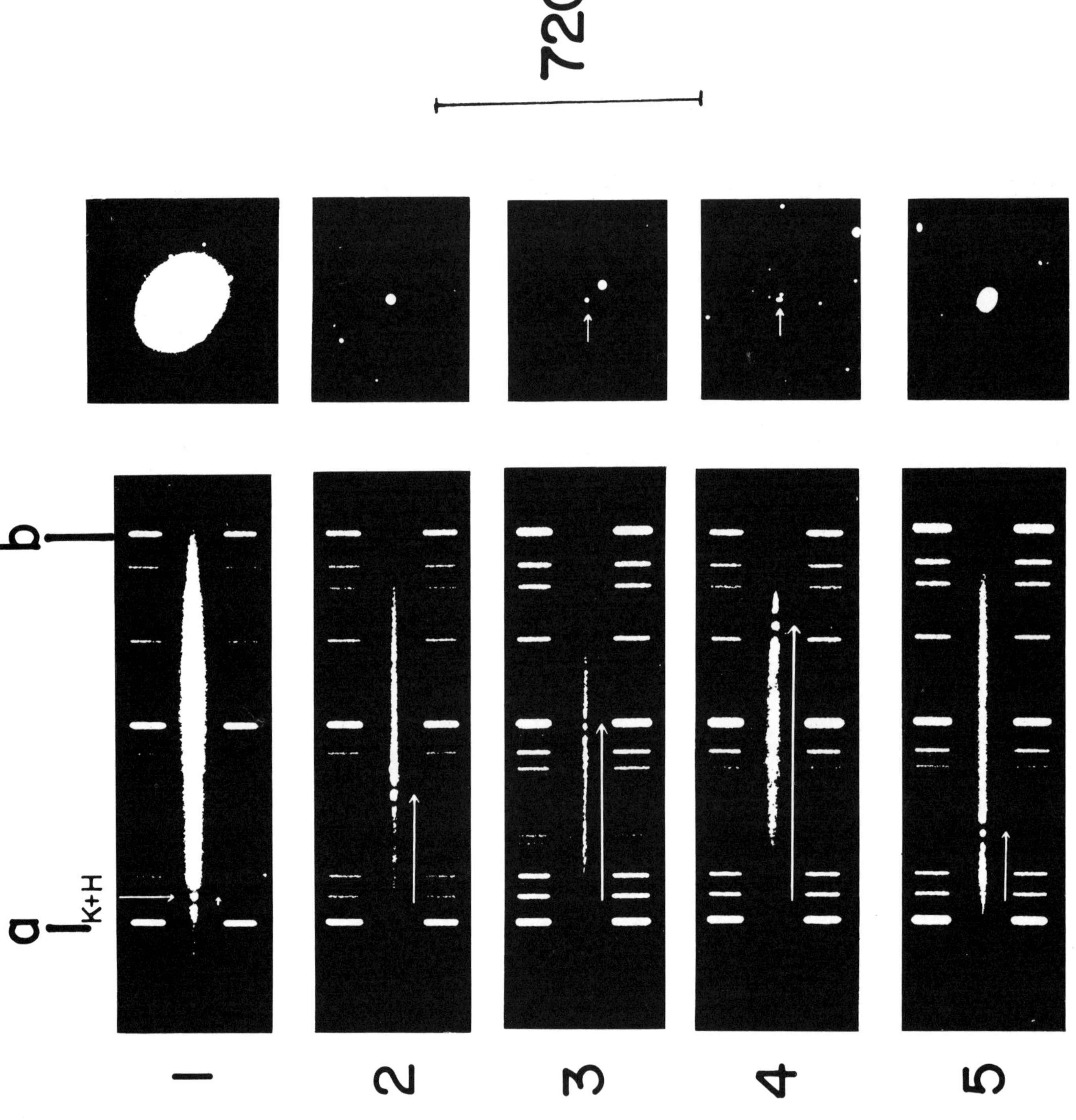

FIGURE 19.1

III. Reductions

Calculate the distance r to each of the galaxies in Figure 19.1, using the relation

$$(19.1) \qquad r = \frac{2.06 \times 10^5}{720} \frac{d_o}{d_G} D_o$$

where D_o is the mean diameter of a bright galaxy and is roughly 3×10^4 pc. Enter your results in your data sheet.

For each galaxy spectrum shown in Figure 19.1, determine the observed wavelengths λ_{Hobs} and λ_{Kobs} from the relations

$$(19.2) \qquad \begin{aligned} \lambda_{Hobs} &= \lambda_a + \frac{x_H}{x_o}(\lambda_c - \lambda_a) \\ \lambda_{Kobs} &= \lambda_a + \frac{x_K}{x_o}(\lambda_c - \lambda_a) \end{aligned}$$

where λ_a and λ_b are the wavelengths of the comparison lines a and b and are equal to 3888.52 Å and 5014.95 Å respectively. If $\lambda_{H\ell ab}$ and $\lambda_{K\ell ab}$ are the laboratory wavelengths of the H and K lines of ionized calcium, then the corresponding Doppler shifts of the lines, z_H and z_K, are given by

$$(19.3) \qquad \begin{aligned} z_H &= \frac{\lambda_{Hobs} - \lambda_{H\ell ab}}{\lambda_{H\ell ab}} \\ z_K &= \frac{\lambda_{Kobs} - \lambda_{K\ell ab}}{\lambda_{K\ell ab}} \end{aligned}$$

Respectively, the values for $\lambda_{H\ell ab}$ and $\lambda_{K\ell ab}$ are 3968.47 Å and 3933.67 Å. Using these relations, calculate the z values for both the H and K lines in each of the spectra shown in Figure 19.1.

Average these two values to obtain $\bar{z}$, the mean Doppler shift of the galaxy spectrum. The radial velocity V_r corresponding to a given value of $\bar{z}$ is then

$$(19.4) \quad V_r = \bar{z}\, c$$

where c is the speed of light. Calculate V_r and its associated quantities and enter all of your results in your data sheet.

Plot V_r versus r using V_r as the ordinate. For the sake of convenience, r may be expressed in megaparsecs (Mpc) where 1 Mpc = 10^6 parsecs. The Hubble constant H is defined as the slope of the V_r versus r plot and should be determined from your plot of these quantities. Enter the value you obtain for H in your data sheet and note the uncertainty in your value.

IV. Questions

1. From the results of this exercise, what, if anything, may be concluded about the universe as a whole?

2. Describe how the Hubble law could be used to obtain extragalactic distances. From your estimated uncertainty in the Hubble constant, how accurate would such distance determinations be?

3. From your results, at what distance does the velocity of recession equal the speed of light? What is the significance of this distance?

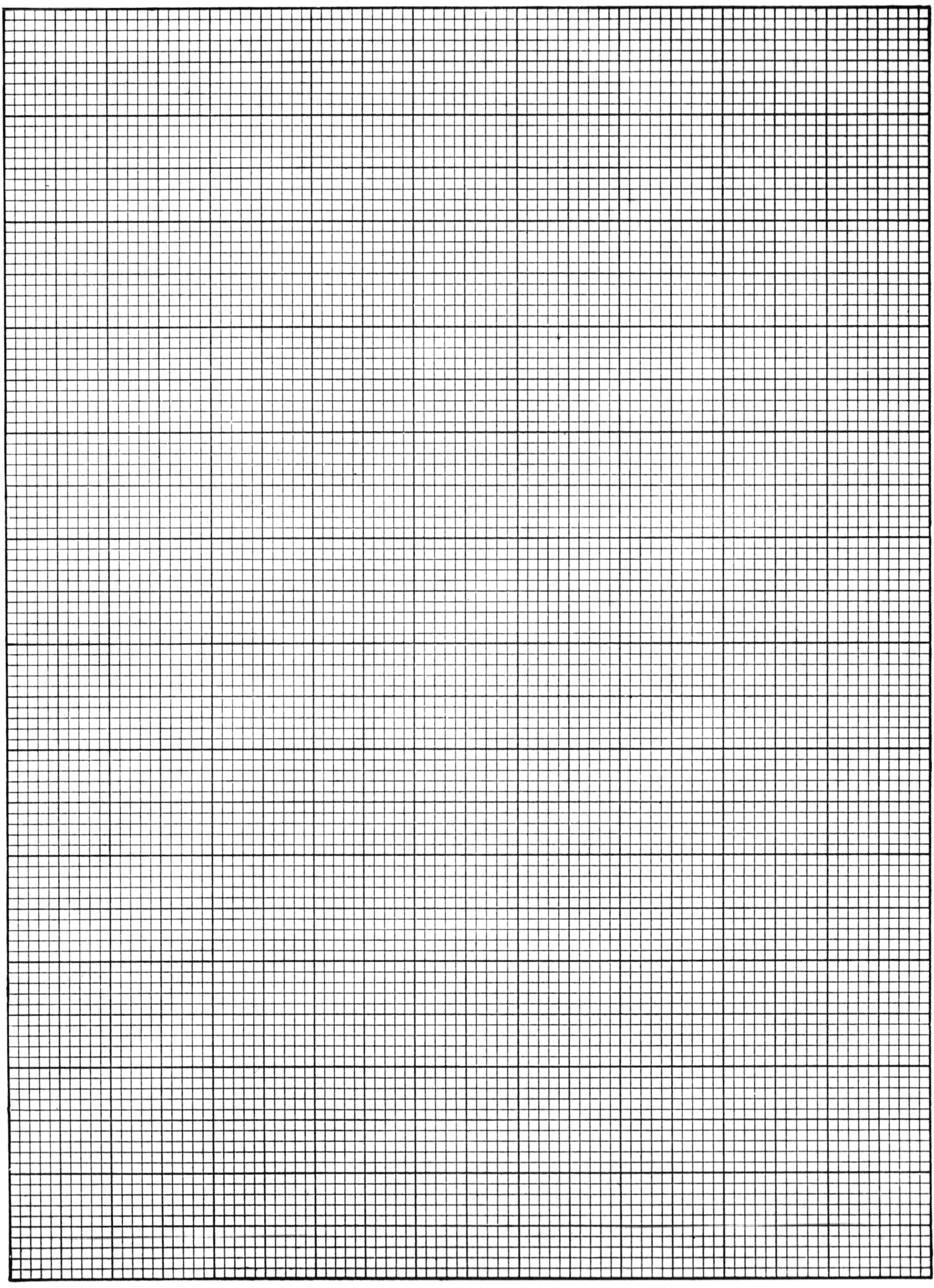

Data Sheet

Galaxy	1	2	3	4	5
d_o(mm)					
d_G(mm)					
r(mpc)					
x_o(mm)					
x_H(mm)					
x_K(mm)					
λ_{Kobs}					
λ_{Hobs}					
$\lambda_{Kobs}-\lambda_{Ko}$					
$\lambda_{Hobs}-\lambda_{Ho}$					
z_K					
z_H					
$\bar{z}$					
V_r(km/sec)					
H(km/sec/Mpc)					

Experiment 20

Gravitational Bending of Starlight

I. Introduction

One of the predicted results of relativity theory is that the path of a light beam can be deflected by the presence of a large gravitational field. For the sun, which possesses the largest gravitational field of any object in the solar system, this effect must be observed during times of total solar eclipse when the solar glare is reduced to the extent that the apparent positions of stars in the vicinity of the sun's disk can be accurately measured. In this exercise, you will investigate the gravitational bending of starlight observed for one such eclipse of the sun.

II. Measurements

Using Figure 20.1, in which the displacements of apparent stellar positions observed during a solar eclipse are displayed as a function of their positions relative to the solar disk, measure the lengths of the displacements x and the corresponding distances d between the center of the solar disk and the "tail" of the displacement. Measure also the length x_o of the 1 arcsecond scaling line as well as the length of the solar diameter d_o. Note that the scaling of the displacement magnitudes is different from that of the positions of the displaced stars relative to the solar disk.

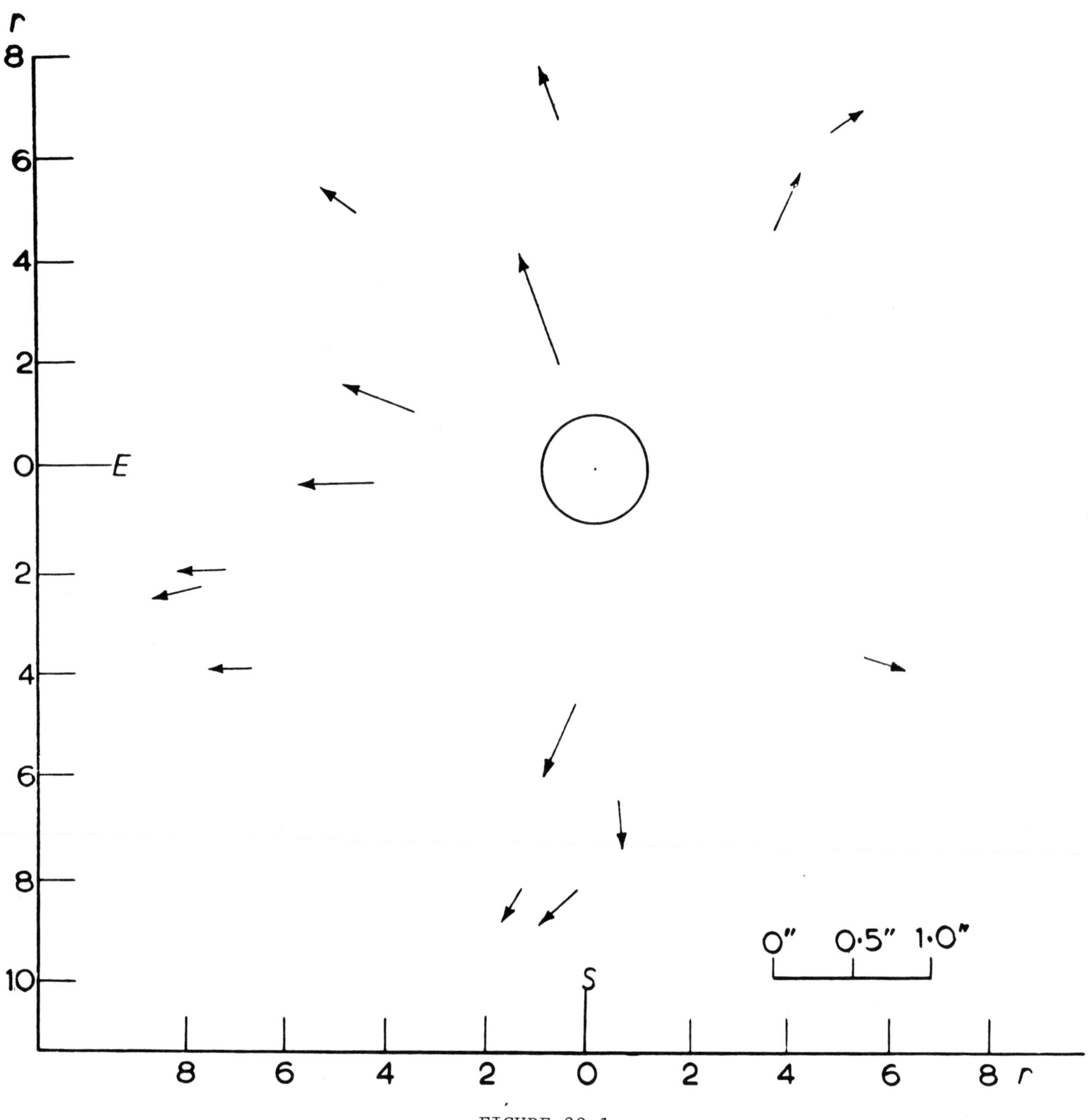

FIGURE 20.1

III. Reductions

Calculate the angular displacement α_* in arcseconds for each star using the relation

$$(20.1) \quad \alpha_* = \frac{x}{x_o}$$

Calculate also the distance r between the center of the sun and each of the measured stars in solar radii using

$$(20.2) \quad r = \frac{2d}{d_o}$$

Enter all of your results in your data sheet.

Plot 1/r versus α using 1/r as the abscissa. Determine the best straight-line fit to the plotted points. From your graph, determine the amount of gravitational bending α_o present at the solar limb (1/r = 1.0). Enter the result in your data sheet.

The displacement α_c in arcseconds of light rays at the solar limb predicted by the classical corpuscular theory of light is

$$(20.3) \quad \alpha_c = 206265 \frac{2GM_\odot}{c^2 R_\odot}$$

while the displacement α_R predicted by relativity theory is

$$(30.4) \quad \alpha_R = 206265 \frac{4GM_\odot}{c^2 R_\odot}$$

Calculate α_c and α_R and enter the results in your data sheet.

IV. Questions

1. Describe how you would experimentally determine the magnitudes of the displacements shown in Figure 20.1.

2. Discuss the advantages and disadvantages of using the moon to measure the gravitational bending of starlight.

3. Which theoretical displacement, α_c or α_R, most closely agrees with your measured value for α_o? Does the accuracy of your experimental value of α_o allow you to distinguish between the classical and relativistic views of gravity-light interaction?

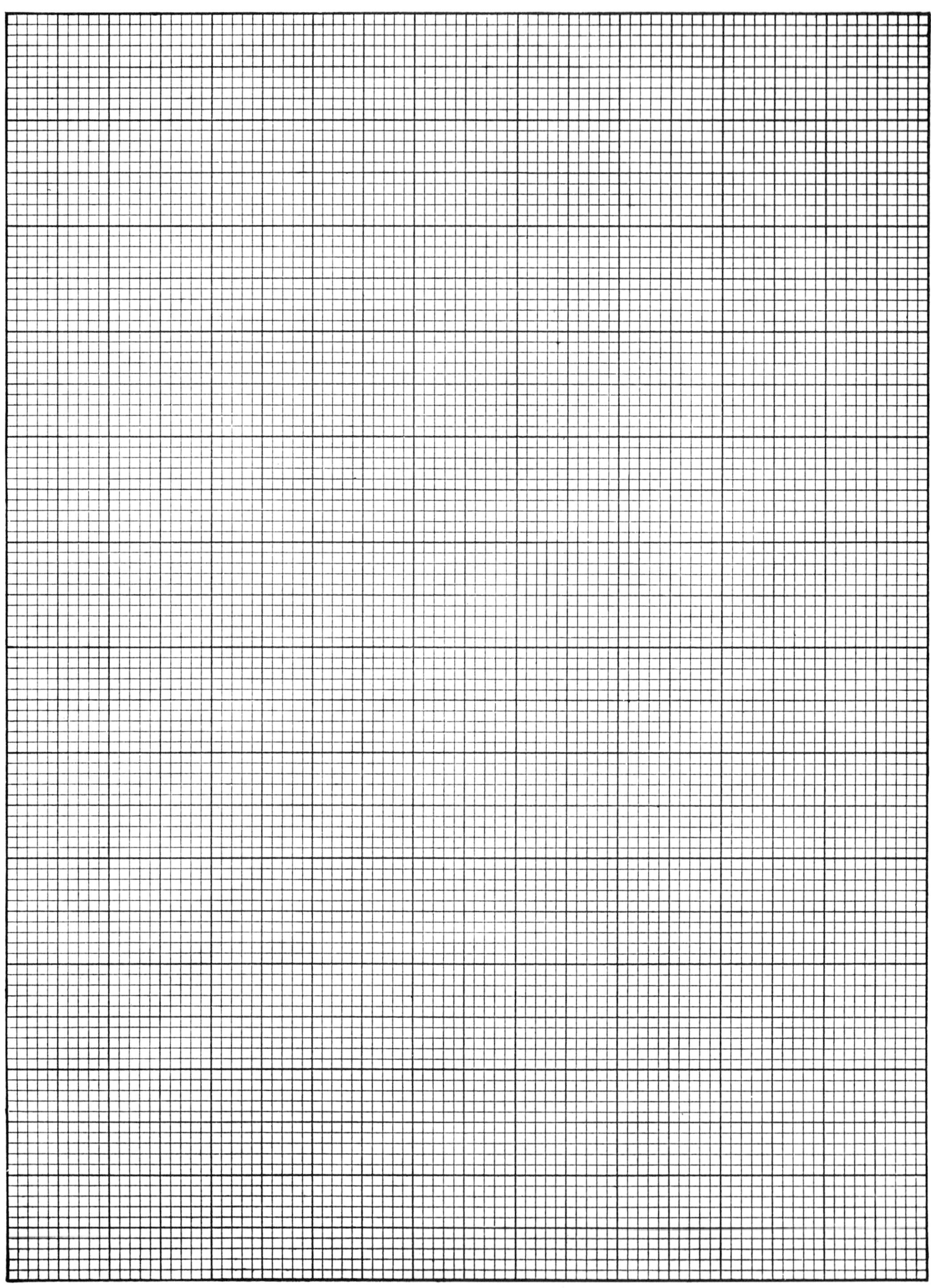

Data Sheet

x_o d_o

Star	x (mm)	α_*	d (mm)	r	$1/r$
1					
2					
3					
4					
5					
6					
7					
8					
9					
10					
11					
12					
13					
14					
15					

α_o

α_c

α_R

Experiment 21

The Crab Nebula Pulsar

I. Introduction

In the summer of 1967, radio astronomers at Cambridge University discovered several radio sources which emit pulses of radio radiation at highly regular time intervals ranging from a few seconds down to small fractions of a second. Studies conducted on these objects, called pulsars, have since indicated that they are stars in the last stages of their evolutionary cycle which have become highly compacted "neutron stars". One of these objects, the Crab Nebula Pulsar (NP 0532) has also been observed in the visual region of the spectrum, and in this exercise you will investigate some of the properties of this amazing object.

II. Measurements

Measure the diameter d of the image of the Crab Nebula Pulsar on each of the photographs shown in Figure 21.1. If the image is not present in a given frame, record zero as the value for d. Enter all of your results in your data sheet.

III. Reductions

Plot the values of d you obtained versus their corresponding time using the time values listed in Table 21.1. Sketch a smooth curve through the resulting points and determine the times at which the diameter of the pulsar image reaches its maximum value.

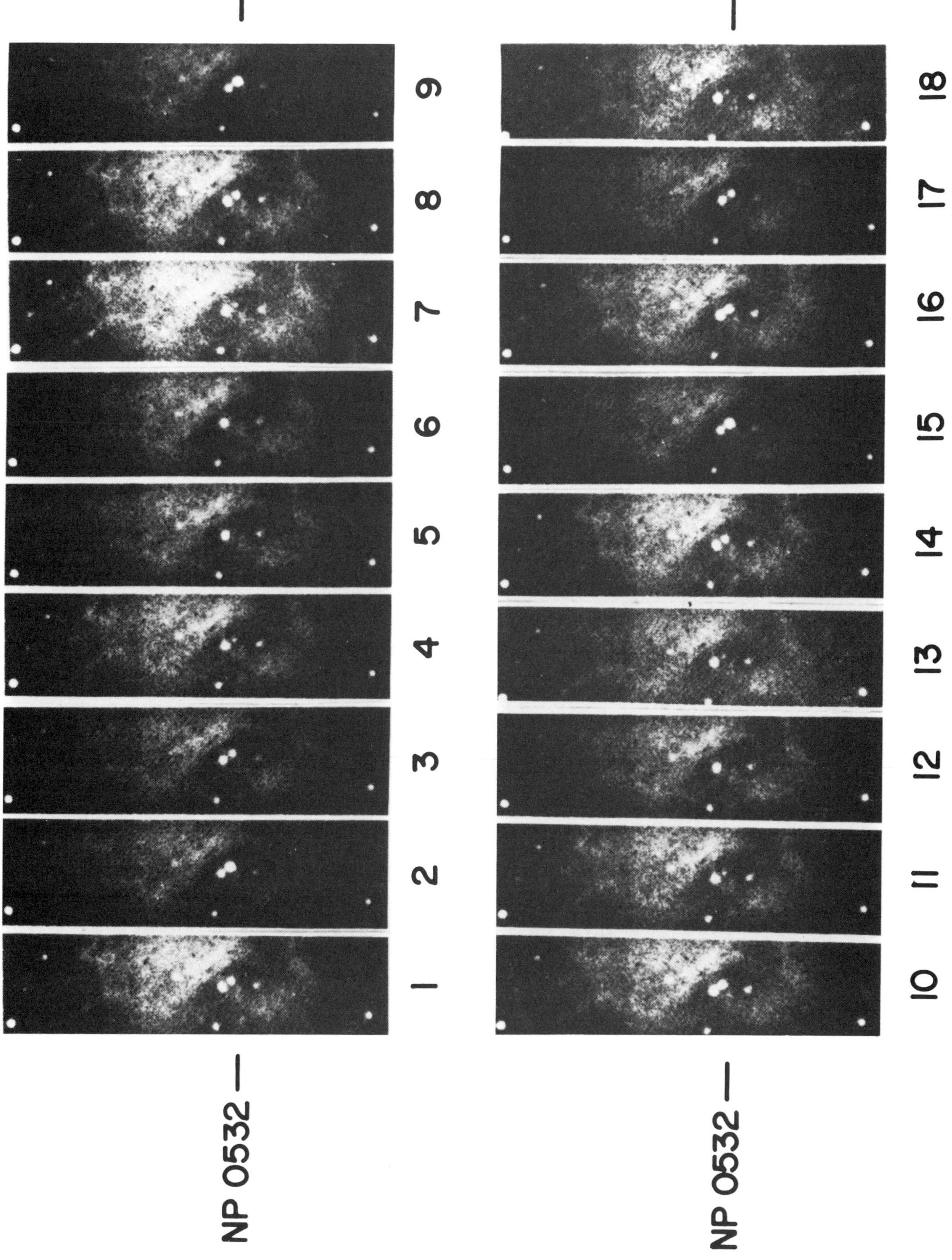

FIGURE 21.1

Table 21.1

Frame	Time (sec)	Frame	Time (sec)
1	.000	10	.045
2	.005	11	.050
3	.010	12	.055
4	.015	13	.060
5	.020	14	.065
6	.025	15	.070
7	.030	16	.075
8	.035	17	.080
9	.040	18	.085

Record the time t_1 of the first maximum and the time t_f of the final maximum. Determine N the number of complete pulsar cycles that have occurred between times t_1 and t_f. Enter your results in your data sheet.

Compute the mean period P of the pulsar variation from the relation

$$(21.1) \quad P = \frac{t_f - t_1}{N}$$

and enter your result in your data sheet.

If the centrifugal forces at the equator of a spherical rotating object are to be balanced by the forces of self-gravity, thereby maintaining the object, the object's mass density ρ must be given by

$$(21.2) \quad \rho = \frac{3\pi}{G}\frac{1}{P^2}$$

where G is the universal gravitation constant, P is the rotation period in seconds, and ρ is the density in $grams/cm^3$. Assuming that the light variation does indeed arise from rotation, calculate the density required for the Crab Nebula Pulsar to gravitationally hold itself together and enter your results in your data sheet. Assuming further that the mass M of this object is about one solar mass or 2×10^{33} grams, estimate the radius R of the pulsar from the relation

$$(21.3) \quad R = \sqrt[3]{\frac{3M}{4\pi\rho}}$$

and enter your results in your data sheet.

The velocity v_e required to escape the surface of the pulsar is

$$(21.4) \quad v_e = \sqrt{\frac{2GM}{R}}$$

Assuming once more that the mass of the pulsar is equal to that of the sun, calculate v_e for the Crab Nebula Pulsar and enter your results in your data sheet, noting how the value you obatin compares with the speed of light c.

IV. Questions

1. What mechanisms other than rotation can you propose to account for the light variation displayed by the Crab Nebula Pulsar?

2. Compare your calculated value of ρ with the densities of materials here on the earth. How does it compare with the densities of other celestial objects?

3. At what radius would the Crab Nebula Pulsar's escape velocity equal the speed of light? What is the significance of such an object?

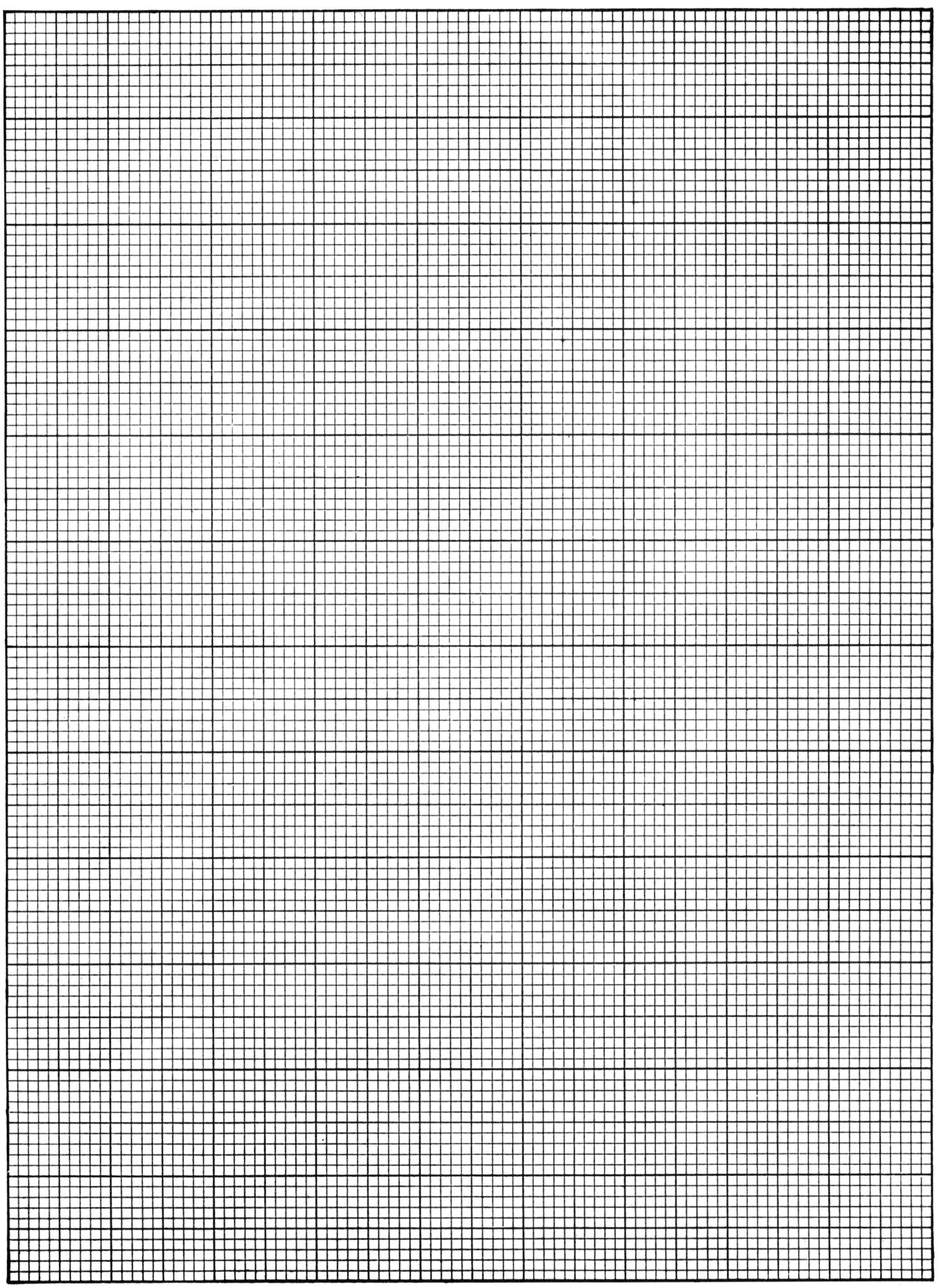

Data Sheet

Frame	Time (sec)	d (mm)
1		
2		
3		
4		
5		
6		
7		
8		
9		
10		
11		
12		
13		
14		
15		
16		
17		
18		

t_1

t_f

N

P

ρ

R

v_e

Experiment 22

Observations of a Quasar

I. Introduction

During the course of the investigation of radio sources in the late 1950's, astronomers discovered several objects exhibiting radio emission which, unlike previously observed sources, displayed only star-like images when photographed at visible wavelengths. Further investigations of these objects, called quasi-stellar radio sources or quasars, have shown them to be among the most puzzling phenomena in the entire universe. In this exercise you will investigate some of the properties of one such quasar, an object designated as PKS 0229 +13.

II. Measurements

On the spectrum of the quasar shown in Figure 22.1, measure the distance x_o between the iron comparison lines at 3889 Å and 5015 Å as well as the distance x_c between the carbon IV emission line and the iron comparison line at 3889 Å. Also measure the distance x_H between the hydrogen Lyman-α line (Ly-α) and the 3889 Å iron comparison line (see Appendix 7).

Measure also the diameters d_i of each of the numbered comparison stars shown in Figure 22.2 as well as the diameter d_Q of the image of PKS 0229 +13 (image "Q"). Enter all of your results in your data sheet.

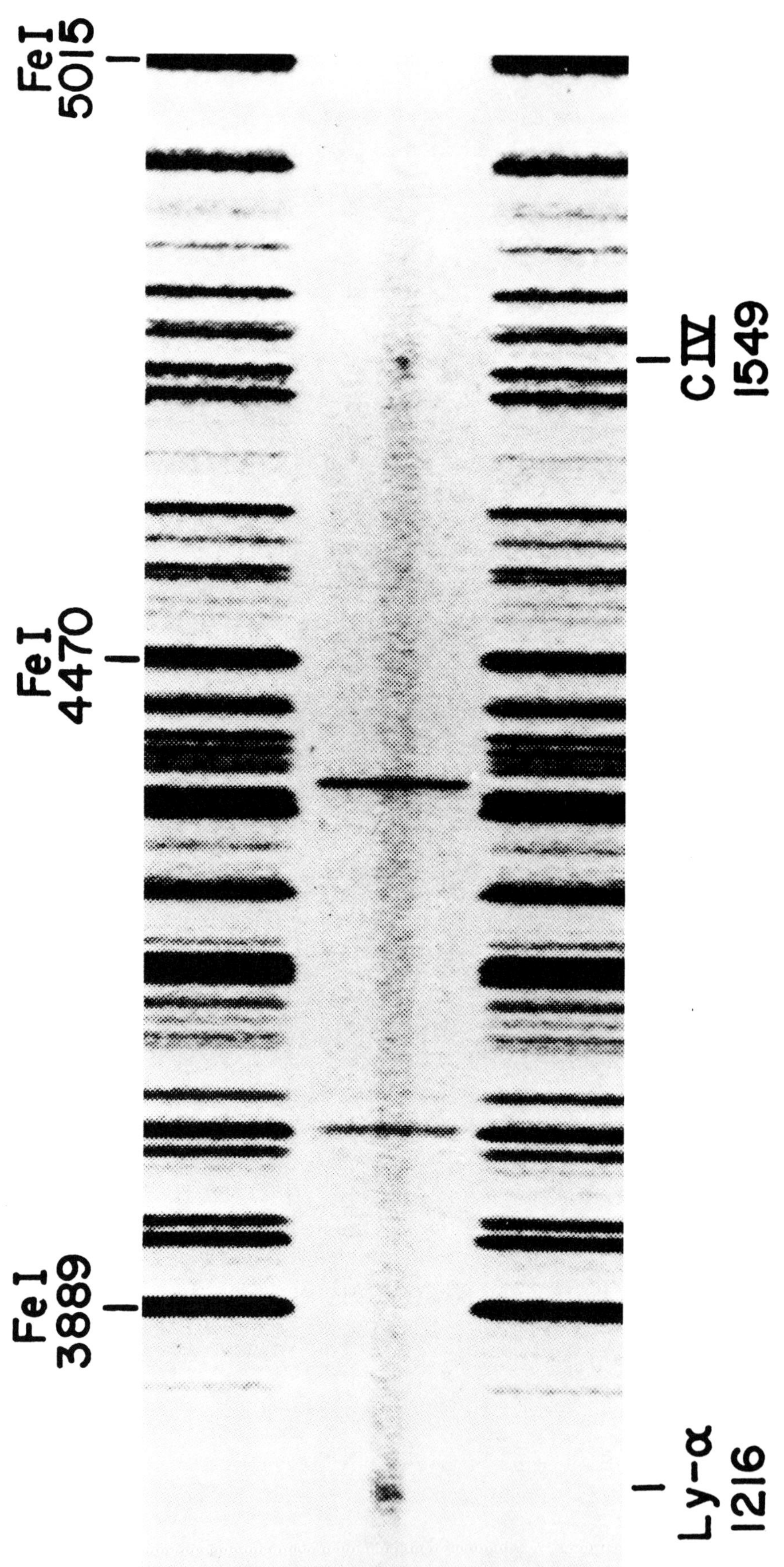

FIGURE 22.1

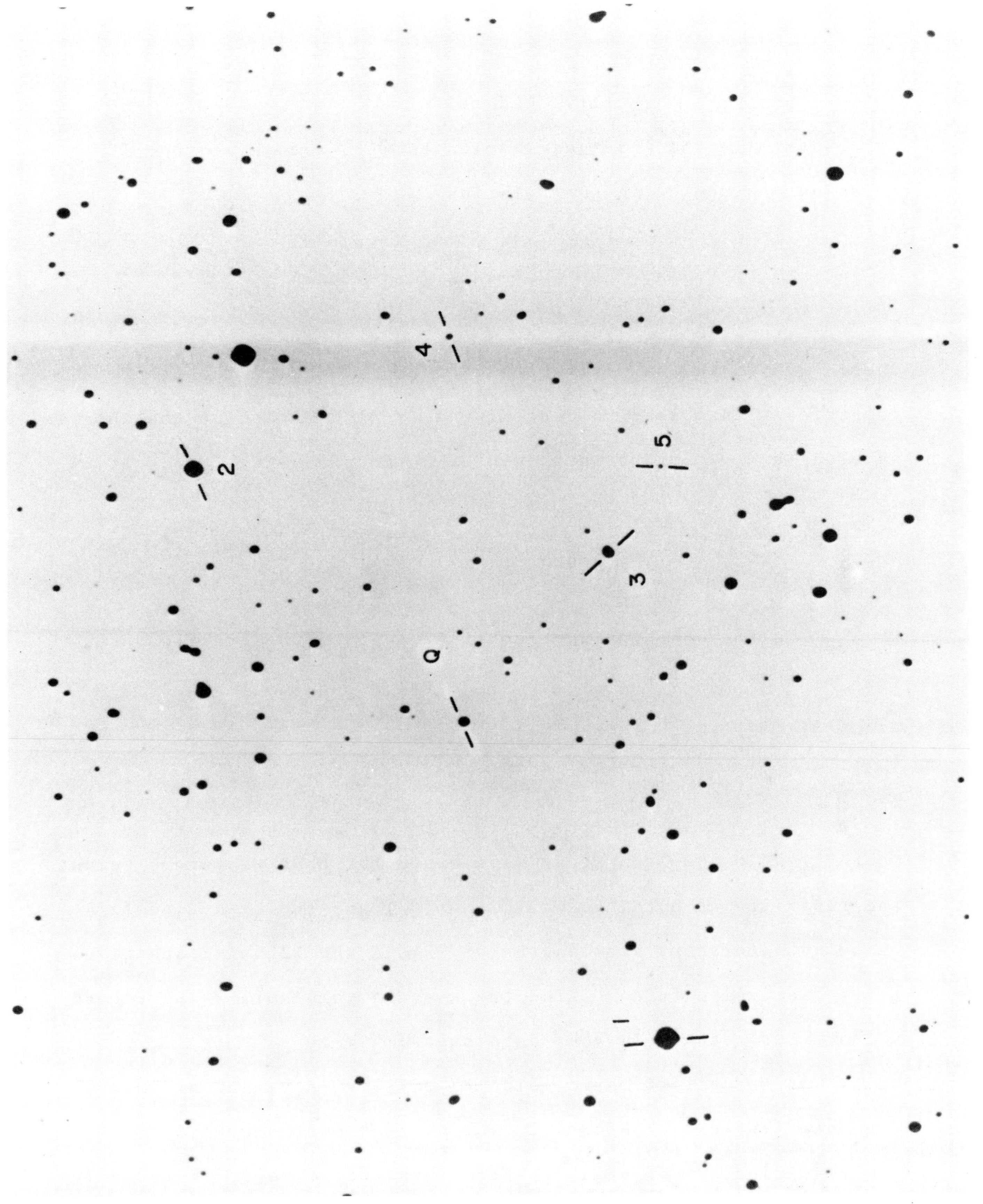

FIGURE 22.2

III. Reductions

Determine the observed wavelength λ_{obsc} of the carbon IV emission feature using the relation

$$(22.1) \quad \lambda_{obsc} = 3889 \text{ Å} + \frac{\lambda_2 - \lambda_1}{x_o} x_c$$

where $\lambda_2 - \lambda_1$ is the wavelength difference between the iron comparison lines used to determine x_o. Also determine the observed wavelength λ_{obsH} of the hydrogen Ly-α feature using the relation

$$(22.2) \quad \lambda_{obsH} = 3889 \text{ Å} - \left[\frac{\lambda_2 - \lambda_1}{x_o}\right] x_H$$

If λ_{obs} is the observed wavelength of a given spectral feature, the redshift z of that feature is defined as

$$(22.3) \quad z = \frac{\lambda_{obs} - \lambda_{lab}}{\lambda_{lab}}$$

where λ_{lab} is the laboratory wavelength for that feature. Compute the redshifts of both the C IV line (z_c) and the Ly-α Line (z_H) assuming laboratory wavelengths of 1549 Å and 1216 Å respectively for these two features. Find the average value of z, and record all of your results in your data sheet.

Plot the relativistic velocity ratio V_r/c versus z, using the data listed in Table 22.1, and pass a smooth curve through the resulting set of points. From your graph, read off the value of V_r/c corresponding to the $\bar{z}$ value obtained for the quasar. If we assume that the redshift of PKS 0229 +13 is cosmological, then the distance r in megaparsecs (1 megaparsec = 1 Mpc = 10^6 pc) to

Table 22.1

The Redshift-Radial Velocity Relation for Relativistic Velocities

V_r/c	z
0.10	1.10
0.20	1.23
0.30	1.37
0.40	1.53
0.50	1.74
0.60	2.00
0.70	2.48
0.80	3.00
0.90	4.36
0.95	6.25

Table 22.2

Magnitude Data for the Comparison Stars

Star	m
1	15.9
2	16.7
3	17.5
4	19.0
5	19.8

this object is given by the Hubble Law

$$(22.3) \quad r = \frac{V_r}{H}$$

where H, the Hubble constant, can be taken to be approximately 100 km/sec/Mpc. Calculate r and enter the result in your data sheet.

Determine the values of d_i^2 and $\log_{10}(d_i^2)$ for each of the comparison stars measured in Section II, and plot the resulting values for $\log_{10}(d_i^2)$ versus their corresponding apparent magnitudes, using the data listed in Table 22.2. Pass a straight line through the resulting set of points. From this calibration line, read off the value of m_Q, the apparent magnitude of the quasar that corresponds to the value of $\log_{10}(d_Q^2)$.

The absolute magnitude M_Q of the quasar can then be obtained from the distance modulus formula

$$(22.4) \quad M_Q = m_Q - 5 \log_{10} r + 5$$

Calculate the absolute magnitude of the quasar PKS 0229 +13 and enter the result in your data sheet.

IV. Questions

1. Compare the absolute magnitude of PKS 0229 +13 with that of (a) the sun, (b) the most luminous stars, and (c) a bright galaxy.

2. If PKS 0229 +13 has a tangential velocity roughly equal to its radial velocity, and proper motions as small as 0.001"/yr can be detected with present instrumentation, how far away must this object be for it to display no detectable proper motion?

3. Aside from its absolute magnitude, how does PKS 0229 +13 differ from a normal galaxy?

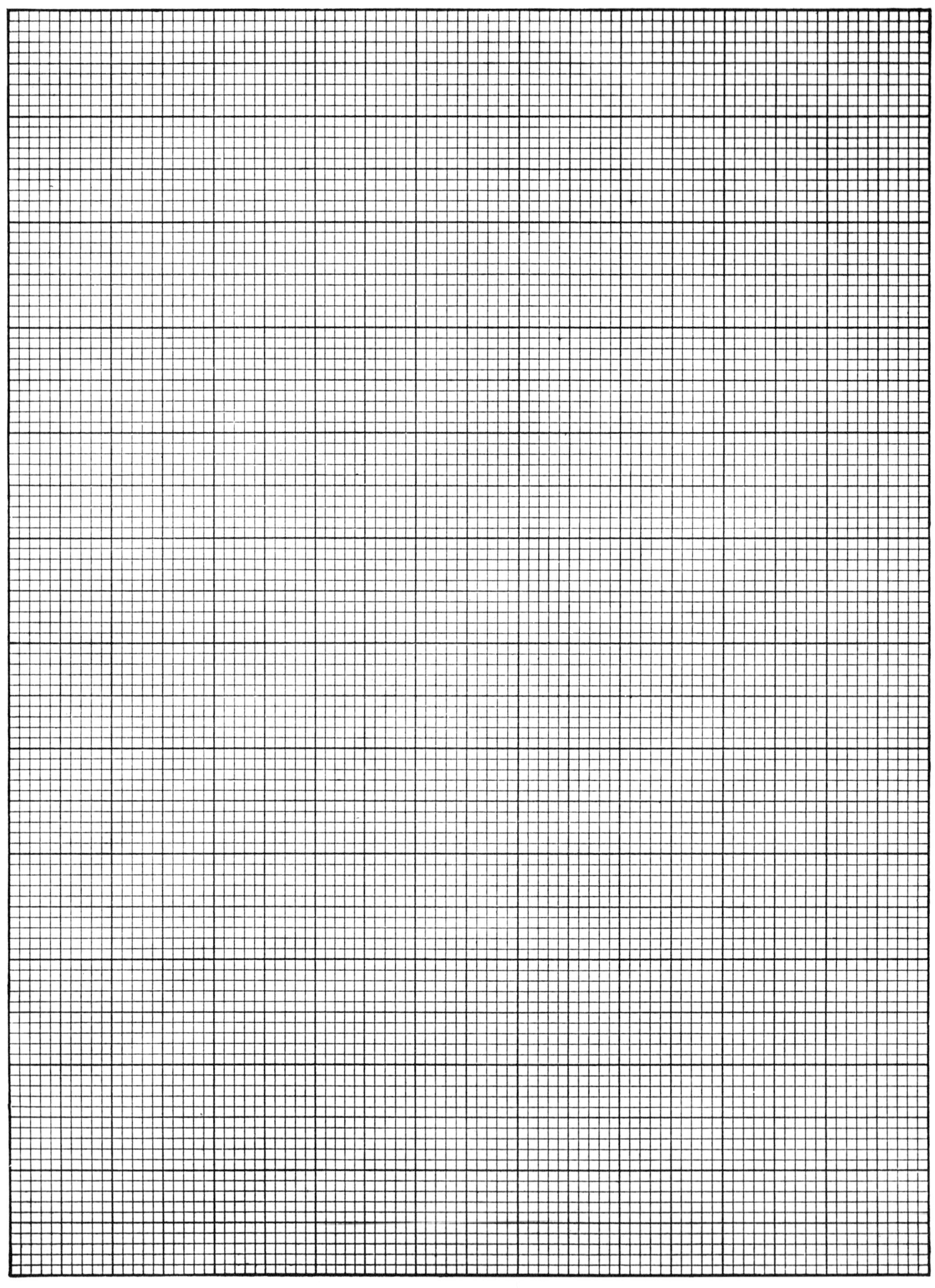

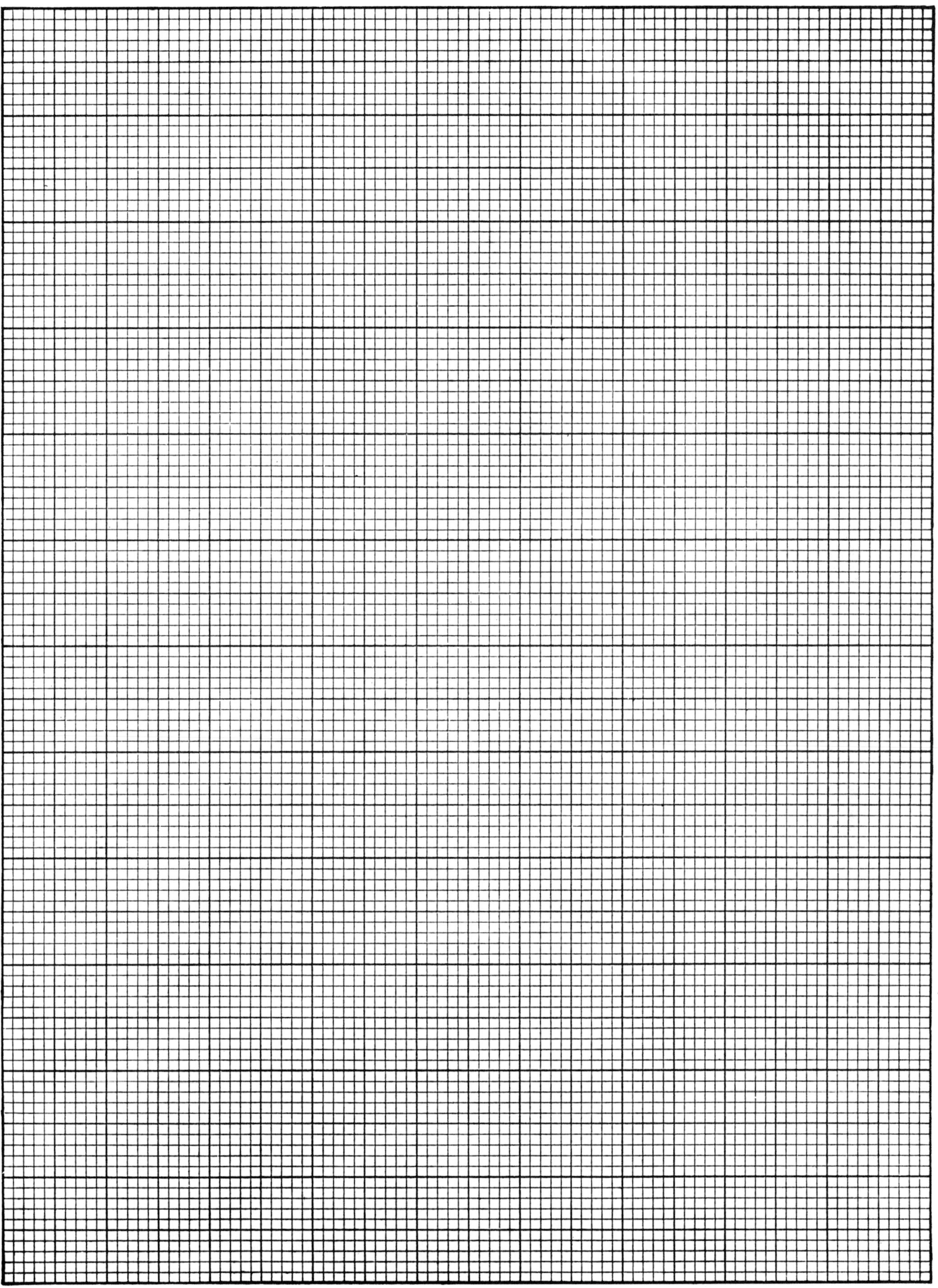

Data Sheet

x_o	x_o
x_c	x_H
λ_{obsc}	λ_{obsH}
z_c	z_H
$\bar{z}$	
V_r	
r	

Star	d (mm)	d^2	$\log_{10}(d^2)$
1			
2			
3			
4			
5			
Q			

m_Q

M_Q

Appendix 1

Some Physical and Astronomical Constants

Astronomical Unit	1 AU = 1.496×10^{13} cm
Sidereal Year	1 yr = 3.156×10^{7} sec
Mass of the Sun	$M_\odot = 1.991 \times 10^{33}$ gm
Luminosity of the Sun	$L_\odot = 3.86 \times 10^{33}$ erg/sec
Radius of the Sun	$R_\odot = 6.960 \times 10^{10}$ cm
Velocity of Light	$c = 2.999 \times 10^{10}$ cm/sec
Mass of the Hydrogen Atom	$m_H = 1.673 \times 10^{-24}$ gm
Stefan-Boltzmann Constant	$\sigma = 5.669 \times 10^{-5}$ erg/cm^2-deg^4-sec
Wien's Law Constant	w = 0.2898 cm-deg
Boltzmann Constant	$k = 1.380 \times 10^{-16}$ erg/deg
Gravitation Constant	$G = 6.668 \times 10^{-8}$ dyne·cm^2/gm^2

Appendix 2

Scientific Notation

In performing numerical computations using the so-called scientific notation, one takes advantage of the fact that every real number can be expressed as the product of some number between one and ten times ten to some power. Thus 200 can be written as 2.0×10^2, 0.4 as 4.0×10^{-1} and so on. The power of ten denotes the number of places that the decimal point must be moved in order to express the given set of significant figures as a number between one and ten. The sign of the exponent on 10 depends on the direction one must move the decimal point. The sign is negative if the direction is to the right and positive if to the left. Thus, 3000 can be expressed as a number between one and ten if we move the decimal point three places to the left, and the number 3000 expressed in scientific notation is then 3.0×10^3. As a second example, the number .00045 in scientific notation is expressed as 4.5×10^{-4}.

The purpose of such notation is to take advantage of the algebraic laws of exponents:

Law	Example
$x^a \cdot x^b = x^{a+b}$	$x^2 \cdot x^3 = x^{2+3} = x^5$
$\dfrac{x^a}{x^b} = x^{a-b}$	$\dfrac{x^4}{x^2} = x^{4-2} = x^2$
	or

$$\frac{x^2}{x^5} = x^{2-5} = x^{-3}$$

$$(x^a)^b = x^{ab} \qquad (x^2)^4 = x^{2\cdot 4} = x^8$$

$$\left(\frac{x}{y}\right)^a = \frac{x^a}{y^a} \qquad \left(\frac{x}{y}\right)^3 = \frac{x^3}{y^3}$$

$$(xy)^a = x^a y^a \qquad (xy)^2 = x^2 y^2$$

$$\sqrt[a]{x} = x^{1/a} \qquad \sqrt[3]{x} = x^{1/3}$$

For example, 8100 divided by .00009 can be calculated rather simply by first writing both numbers in scientific notation as follows:

$$\frac{8100}{0.00009} = \frac{8.1 \times 10^3}{9.0 \times 10^{-5}} = 0.9 \times 10^{3-(-5)}$$

$$= 0.9 \times 10^{+8}$$

$$= 9 \times 10^{-1} \times 10^{+8}$$

$$= 9 \times 10^{8-1}$$

$$= 9 \times 10^7$$

The method can be extended even further through the use of a table of logarithms (see Appendix 8) in which numbers between one and ten are expressed as a power of ten. Thus the problem 434 × .00313 is solved as follows:

$$434 \times 0.00313$$

$$(4.34 \times 10^{2}) \times (3.13 \times 10^{-3})$$

$$(10^{.637} \times 10^{2}) \times (10^{.496} \times 10^{-3})$$

$$(10^{2.637}) \times (10^{-2.504})$$

$$10^{2.637-2.504}$$

$$10^{.133}$$

or

$$1.36$$

The logarithm of a number is defined as the power to which ten must be raised in order to produce the number. In the above example the logarithms of 434 and 0.00313 are, respectively, 2.637 and -2.550.

Appendix 3

The "Fat" Triangle

One of the theorems of plane geometry states that if two triangles are similar, i.e., have the same set of angles, then one triangle is simply an enlargement or scaled up version of the other. In particular, for any right triangle, the ratio of the lengths of two of the sides of the triangle depend solely on the sizes of the two acute angles in the triangle. Mathematicians have thus developed a set of so-called trigonometric functions which are defined in terms of ratios of the sides of the triangle as follows:

$$\text{sine}(\theta) = \sin\theta = \frac{\text{side opposite angle }\theta}{\text{hypotenuse}}$$

$$\text{cosine}(\theta) = \cos\theta = \frac{\text{side adjacent angle }\theta}{\text{hypotenuse}}$$

$$\text{tangent}(\theta) = \tan\theta = \frac{\text{side opposite angle }\theta}{\text{side adjacent angle }\theta}$$

Three additional functions are also of interest:

$$\text{secant}(\theta) = \sec\theta = \frac{\text{hypotenuse}}{\text{side adjacent angle }\theta} = \frac{1}{\cos\theta}$$

$$\text{cosecant}(\theta) = \csc\theta = \frac{\text{hypotenuse}}{\text{side opposite angle }\theta} = \frac{1}{\sin\theta}$$

$$\text{cotangent}(\theta) = \cot\theta = \frac{\text{side adjacent angle }\theta}{\text{side opposite angle }\theta} = \frac{1}{\tan\theta}$$

All of the above ratios have the same values for a given angle regardless of the size of the triangle involved and can hence be tabulated as a function of the angle (see Appendix 9). This invariant property of the trigonometric functions makes them

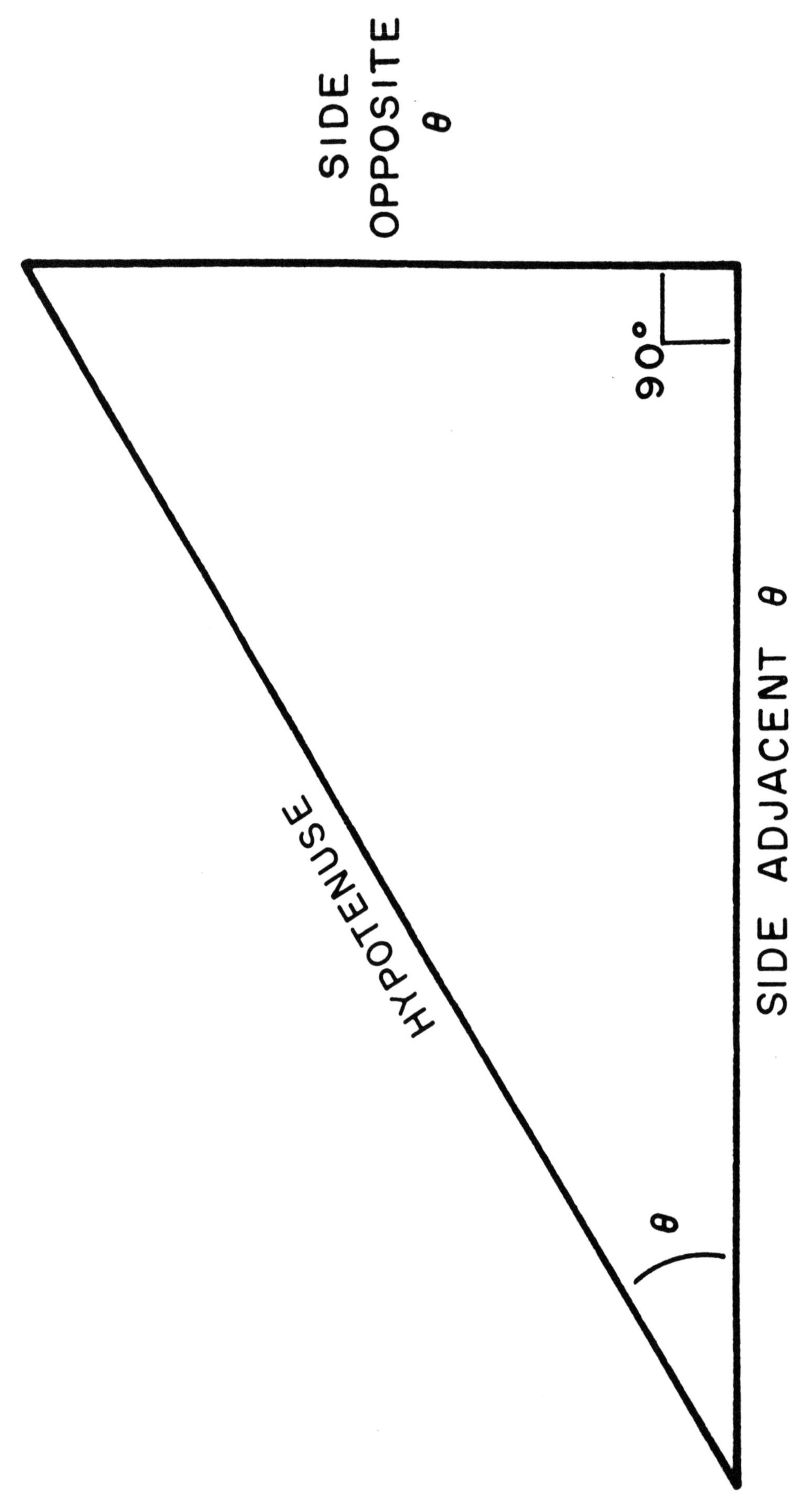

FIGURE A3.1

extremely useful in a wide variety of calculations, including some of those encountered in observational astronomy. For example, suppose two observers separated by 150 miles as shown in Figure A3.2 observe an artificial satellite. If one observer sees the satellite directly overhead and the second observer sees the satellite at an angle of 40 degrees above the horizon, what is the satellite's altitude?

By definition,

$$\tan(40°) = \frac{\text{side opposite } 40° \text{ angle}}{\text{side adjacent } 40° \text{ angle}}$$

From Appendix 9, tan 40° = 0.839, and since the adjacent side is 150 miles, we have

$$0.839 = \frac{\text{side opposite } 40° \text{ angle}}{150}$$

where the satellite altitude is the side opposite the 40° angle and is equal to 150 × 0.839 or 126 mi.

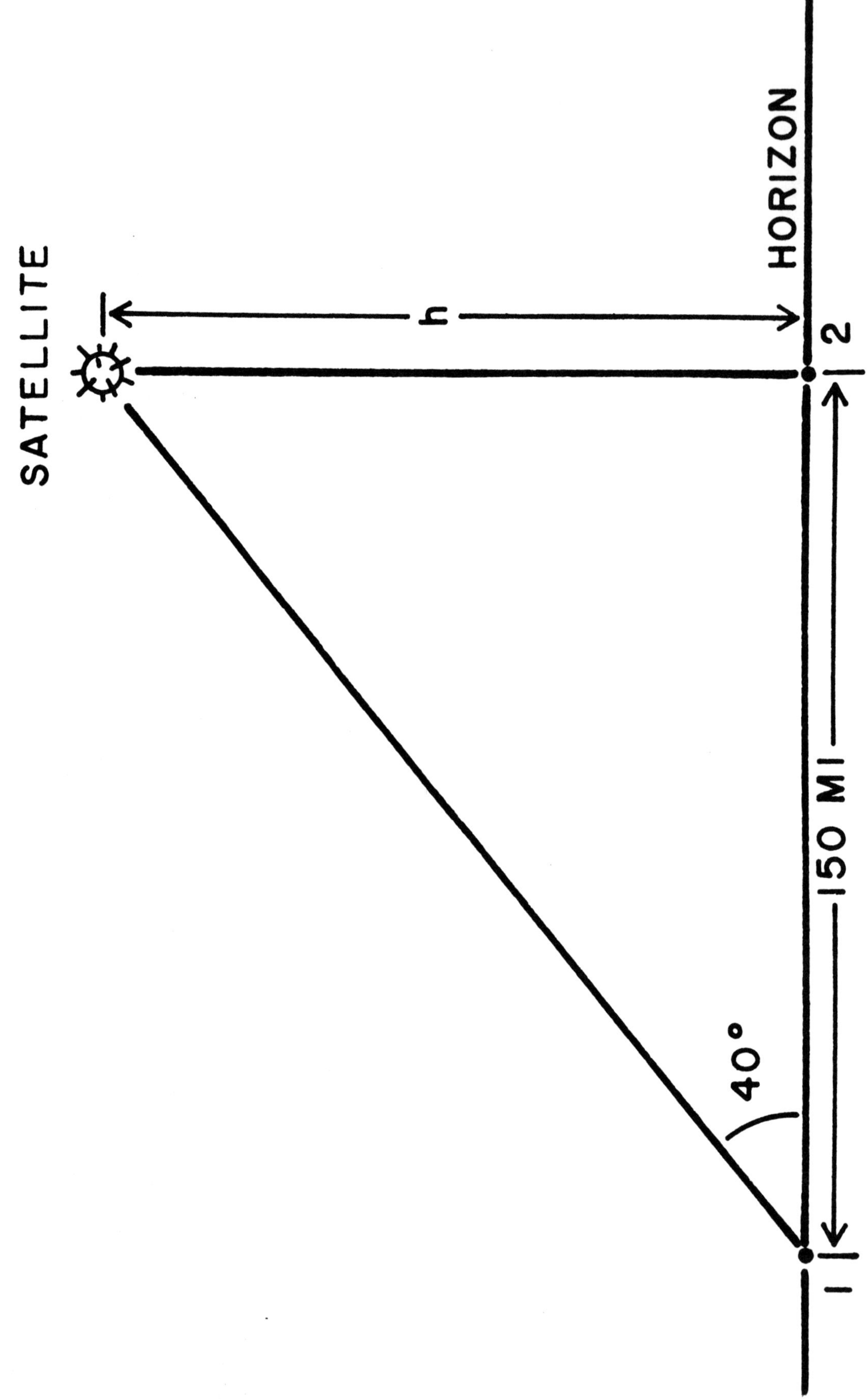

FIGURE A3.2

Appendix 4
The "Thin" Triangle

There are many problems in astronomy involving the so-called "thin" triangle in which two sides are very long compared with the third side (see Figure A4.1). For such a triangle it can be shown that the angle α opposite the short side D is given by

$$\text{(A4.1)} \quad \alpha(\text{arcseconds}) = 206265 \frac{D}{r}$$

where the angle α is measured in arcseconds (one arcsecond = 1/3600 degree) and r and D are in the same units. Additional forms of the above equation which are useful include

$$\text{(A4.2)} \quad D = \frac{\alpha r}{206265}$$

and

$$\text{(A4.3)} \quad r = \frac{206265\ D}{\alpha}$$

These relationships find considerable use in astronomical problems such as the following.

Example: Find the linear diameter of a star cluster 100 parsecs distant which has an observed angular diameter of 2000 arcseconds.

Solution: From Equation A4.2 we have

$$D = \frac{\alpha r}{206265}$$

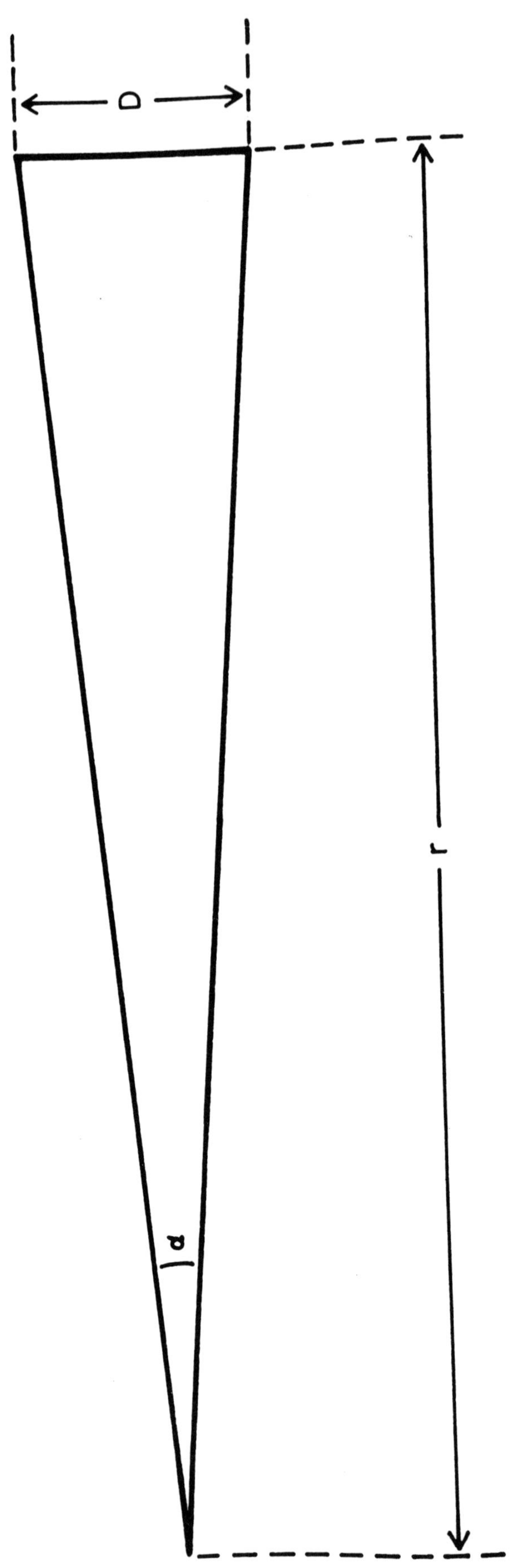

FIGURE A4.1

$$D = \frac{(2\times10^3)(1\times10^3)}{2.06\times10^5}$$

and finally

$$D = 9.7 \text{ parsecs} .$$

Appendix 5

Graphs

In astronomy as well as other branches of science, it is often useful to construct "pictures" or graphs of various relationships. There are a number of coordinate systems in which this can be accomplished, but the most commonly used systems are the so-called Cartesian or rectangular system and the polar system.

The Cartesian system consists of a set of two perpendicular scaled axes, usually called the x and y axes, in which any point on the xy plane is located by specifying its x and y coordinates. By convention the x-axis (abscissa) is set horizontally and the y-axis (ordinate) vertically. The intersection of the axes is said to be the origin of the system and has a position of (0.0). Positive x values are plotted to the right of the origin and positive y values are plotted above the origin (see Figure A5.1).

Like the Cartesian system, the Polar coordinate system also employs two coordinates to describe a point in 2-dimensional space. In this instance, however, the point is located by its distance r from the origin and the angle θ between the + x axis and the line from the origin to the point. The system is much the same as that used by a radar scope to accurately locate a target.

In both instances, the scale of the plot, directions of positive and negative axes, etc., can be altered to fit the data involved. Your instructor will provide the necessary assistance in this regard.

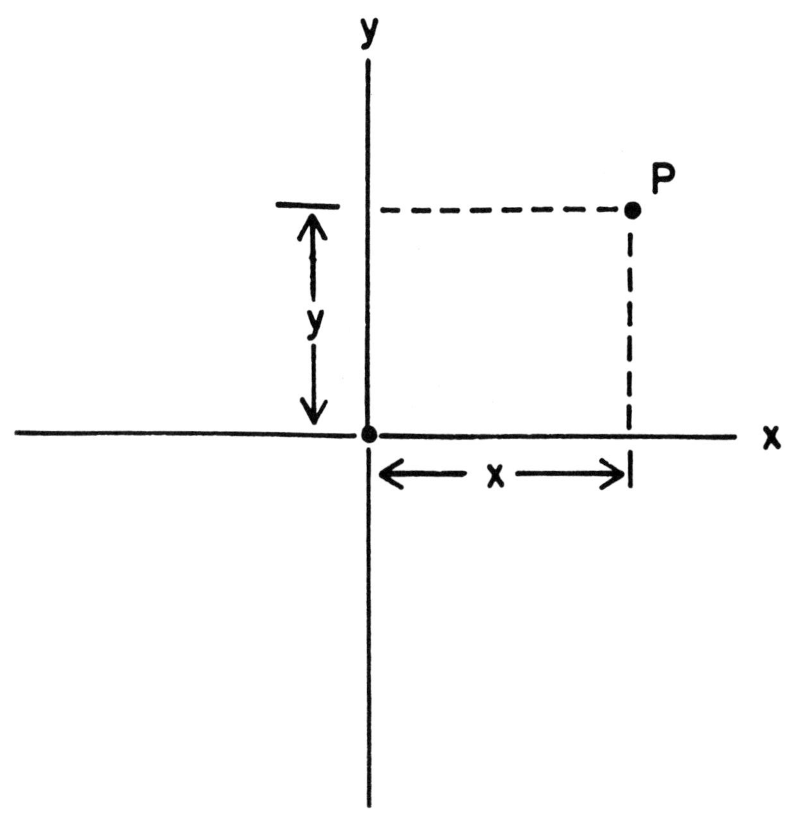

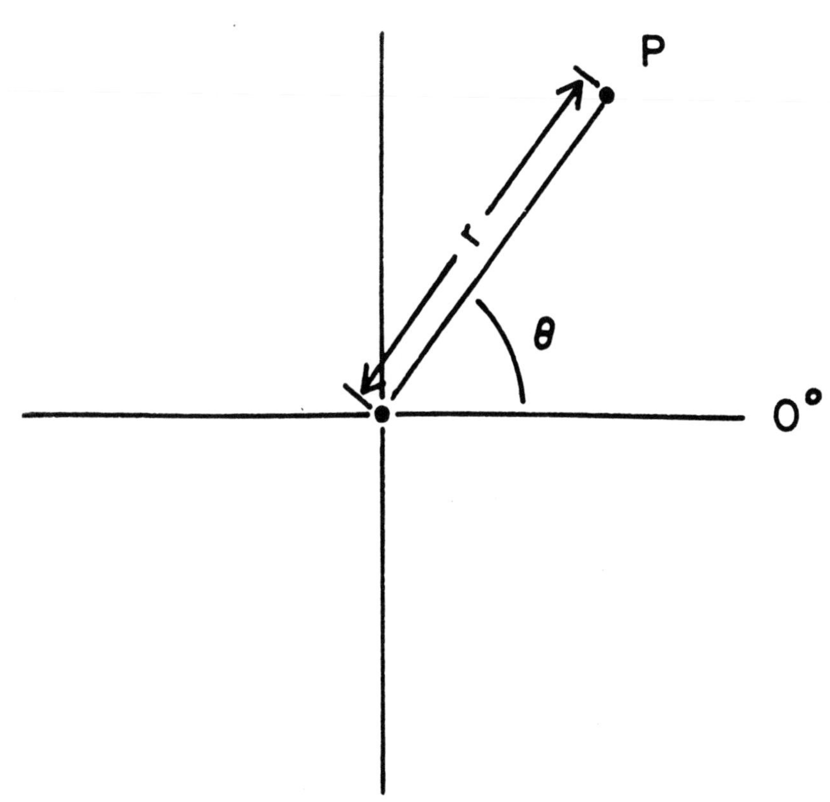

FIGURE A5.1

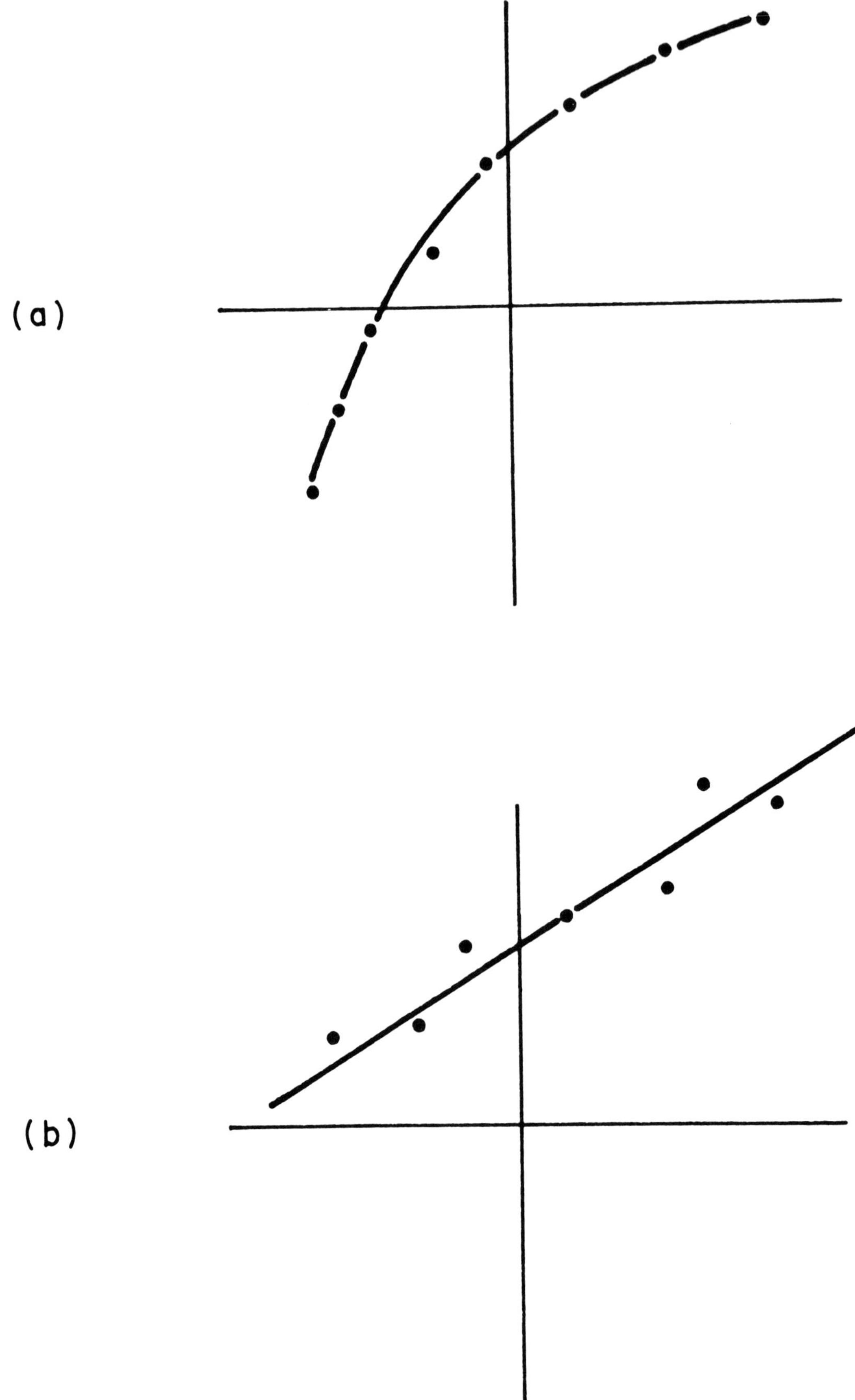

FIGURE A5.2

The actual graph of a relationship is constructed by plotting the given data and then passing a continuous curve through the resulting points. In some instances, the data must be "fit" by a specific type of curve such as a straight line. In this case, the curve is constructed so that the sum total of the distances between the points and the curve is roughly minimized. Two examples of these graphing techniques are shown in Figure A5.2 in which a smooth curve is passed through a set of data points (Figure A5.2a) and a straight line fit is made to a set of data points (Figure A5.2b).

When a straight line is fit to a set of data, an important characteristic of that line is the rate at which the y values rise or fall with x. This characteristic is referred to as the slope of the line. If (x_1, y_1) and (x_2, y_2) are the Cartesian coordinates of two points on a straight line, then the slope of the line is formally defined as follows:

$$\text{(A5.1)} \quad \text{slope} = \frac{y_2 - y_1}{x_2 - x_1}$$

Thus for a line passing through the points (1, 3) and (5, 6) the slope would be (6-3)/(5-1) or 3/4.

Appendix 6

Scaling

There are a number of exercises in this text which rely on the principle of scaling. Perhaps the most familiar example of scaling is its use on maps. Suppose, for example, we wish to determine the distance between point 0 and the lighthouse on the map shown in Figure A6.1. Using scaling techniques, one first measures the distance x_{LH} on the map between point 0 and the lighthouse. Next, the length x_o of the 5 kilometer scaling line is measured in the same units of length as x_{LH}. Since the length x_o corresponds to an actual distance of 5 kilometers, from the principle of scaling, the distance d_{LH} to the lighthouse is thus given by

$$\frac{x_{LH}}{d_{LH}} = \frac{x_o}{5\ \text{km}}$$

or

$$d_{LH} = \frac{x_{LH}}{x_o}\ 5\ \text{km}$$

In this case x_{LH}/x_o is about 0.5, so the actual distance between point 0 and the lighthouse on the same scale would be roughly 2.5 km. In like fashion, the distance between point 0 and the town would be about 4 km and that between point 0 and the waterfall would be about 5 km. Thus, through the use of scaling, measurements made on photographs, maps, etc., can be converted to distances, angular diameters and the like.

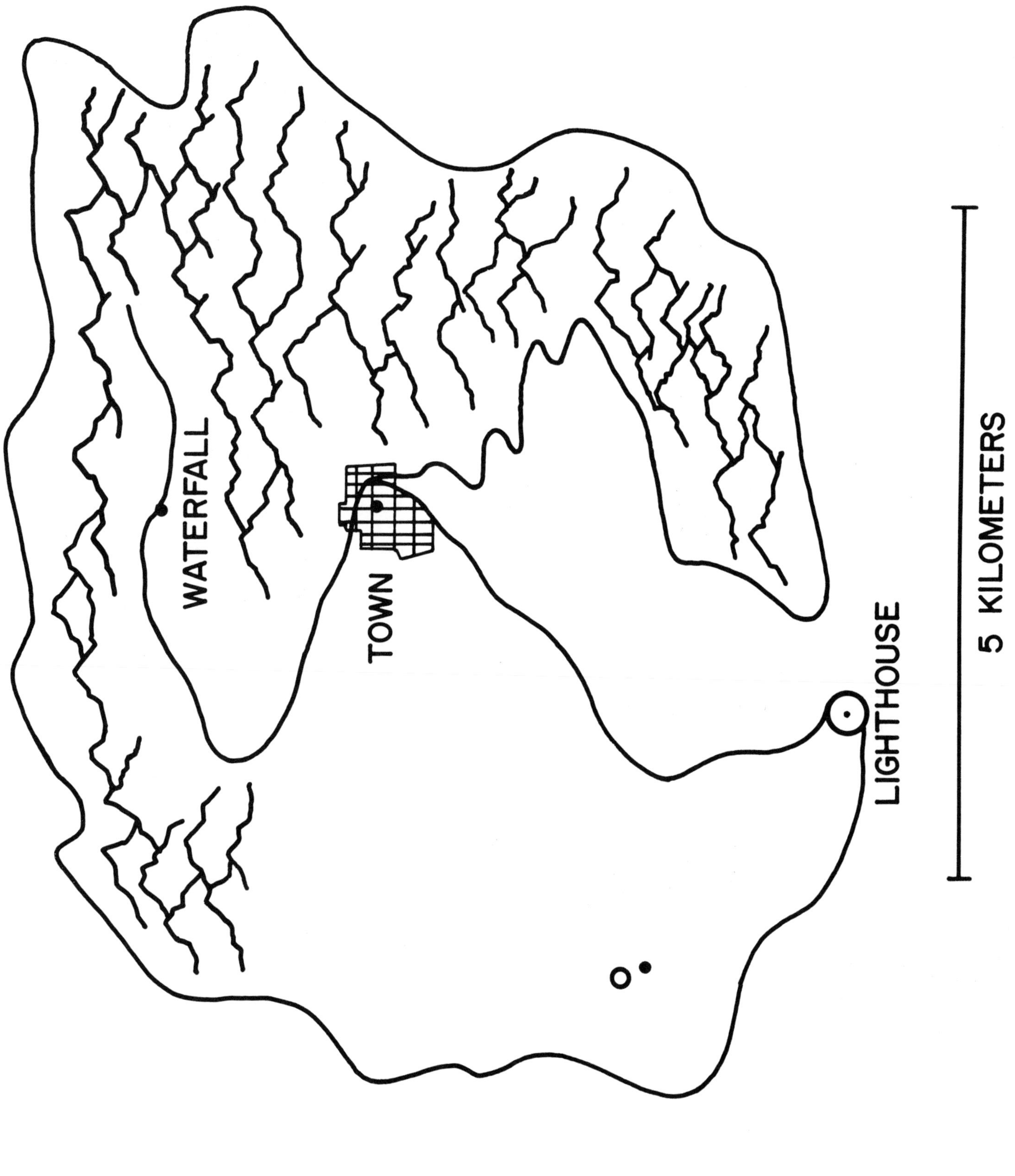

FIGURE A6.1

Appendix 7

Wavelength Determination

Quite often in observational astronomy it is useful to measure the wavelengths of absorption or emission lines which appear in the spectra of celestial objects. When photographing spectra of celestial objects, astronomers also almost always photograph two additional "comparison" spectra in such a way that the comparison spectra bracket the spectrum of the celestial object (see Figure A7.1). The comparison spectrum arises from a source which is at rest relative to the spectrograph and whose composition is known (iron, neon, titanium, etc.). In this way the astronomer is assured that the wavelengths of the comparison spectrum have well determined values which are not altered by the Doppler effect.

If one makes the simple assumption that the scale of a given spectrogram is linear, one can find the wavelength λ_{line} of a given line in the spectrum of the object by first measuring the distance x_o between two comparison lines having known wavelengths λ_1 and λ_2. If the distance x_{line} is also measured then the wavelength of the line of interest is given by

$$\lambda_{line} = \lambda_1 + \frac{x_{line}}{x_o} (\lambda_2 - \lambda_1)$$

Suppose, for example, that the two comparison wavelengths λ_1 and λ_2 are 4000 Å and 5000 Å, respectively, and x_o = 10 cm. If x_{line} for the line of interest is 3 cm, then the value of λ_{line}

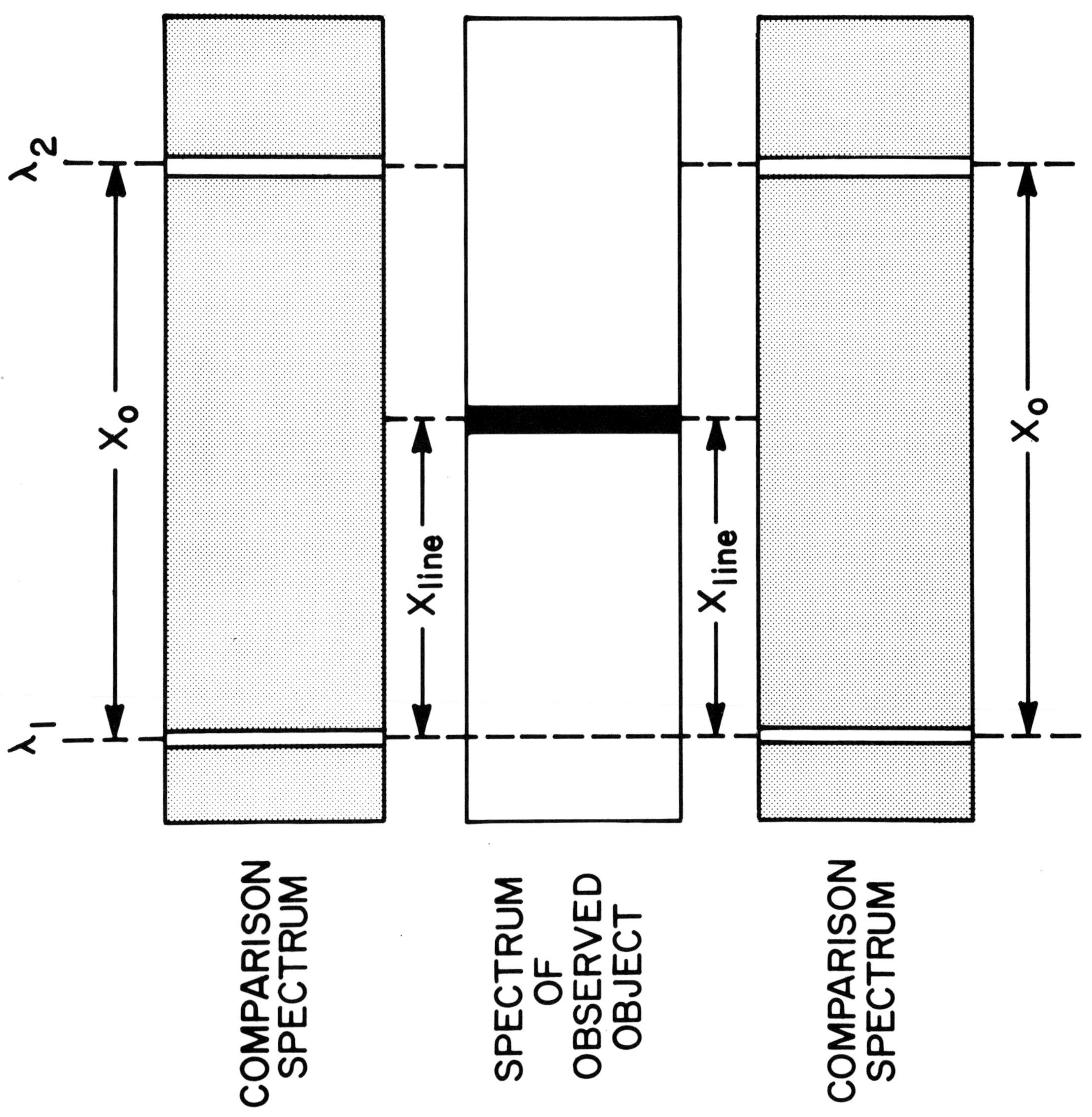
λ2
λ1
Xo
Xline
Xline
Xo
COMPARISON SPECTRUM
SPECTRUM OF OBSERVED OBJECT
COMPARISON SPECTRUM

FIGURE A7.1

would be

$$\lambda_{line} = 4000\ \text{Å} + \frac{3\ \text{cm}}{10\ \text{cm}}\ (5000\ \text{Å} - 4000\ \text{Å})$$

or $\lambda_{line} = 4300$ Å.